Hebridean Waves

Hebridean Waves

Kayaking
Scotland's West Coast

Ewan Gillespie

Cualann Press

ISBN: 978-0-9554273-2-9

First published in 2007

British Library Cataloguing in Publication Data. A catalogue record of
this book is available at the British Library.

Printed by Bell & Bain, Glasgow

Published by:
Cualann Press, 6 Corpach Drive, Dunfermline, KY12 7XG, Scotland
Tel/Fax +44 (0)1383 733724
Email: info@cualann.com
Website: www.cualann.com

Contents

Foreword by Neil Griffiths   vii

Introduction   ix

Chapter 1: Skye, just turn right!   13

Chapter 2: Mull, all the way round, eventually   35

Chapter 3: Lochboisdale to Stornoway   59

Chapter 4: Barra, Mingulay and the Uists   81

Chapter 5: Leverburgh to Callanish, in fog   97

Chapter 6: Eigg, Rum, and almost Canna   111

Chapter 7: Oban to Skipness and Inveraray   121

Chapter 8: Arran, at its best   135

Chapter 9: Islay, Gigha and Colonsay   149

I would like to dedicate this book to my daughter, Cait

Foreword

My first experience of seawater canoeing on Scotland's west coast was physically exhausting but psychologically uplifting. We paddled along the Crinan Canal – saltwater, I suppose – to Ardrishaig, down Loch Fyne, carried our canoes to West Loch Tarbert and ended near Machrihanish. Our three double-canoes had a buoyancy only slightly better than a Clyde puffer and came without spray sheets. Kayaks were posh then. The six of us were all aged fifteen.

That cloudless trip back in '72 left me with a bad case of sunburn, a saltily chaffed neck and a blazing sense of elation. A small adventure, blithely entered, had opened up, it seemed, the whole world. My affection for canoeing and all points between the Butt of Lewis and the Mull of Kintyre began that summer.

Hebridean Waves inevitably puts me in mind of the highs and lows, mostly highs, of canoeing at sea with its happy freedoms and excitements, while all the time enjoying the natural glories of seas and shores. Some of our experiences and those of Ewan Gillespie overlap exactly; we, too, skipped the last locks of the Crinan Canal and carried our canoes to the sea direct. We also shared basking shark scares and the delights of spotting seals and otters in the peculiarly intimate way that only canoes permit. It reminded me of how reviving, in fatigue, a hot coffee can be. Simple pleasures, yes, but simply unforgettable.

Thirty years later I led a group of Gurkhas on a march from the most northerly point of the Outer Hebrides to the most southerly. The boys loved the islands, instinctively recognizing their beauty and culture in an almost mystical way.

Reading *Hebridean Waves* was to revisit those magical places. Ewan Gillespie's detailed account, however, reminds us all, not just me, of what sparkling discoveries await around every headland in the Outer Isles. The seals, puffins, porpoise and breath-taking landscapes combine to present one of the world's most compelling places. To go by kayak brings the visitor even closer to their delights.

Ewan is light on the muscular agonies of first-day paddling, but discomfort is never far away. My Gurkhas never had to face the dangers of high seas meeting outgoing tides, rushing between tooth-like skerries, and we were lucky with the midges. Unlike Ewan, our concerns about ferries focused on their timings, not whether they would appear out of a sea fog and run us down.

Hebridean Waves is more than an account of luxuriating in the glories of Nature and the special thrill of exploring little-known lagoons and inlets. It takes us through the difficulties of navigation, the hazards of big seas and the perils of beaching on frothy, rocky shores when you're tired and numb with cold.

Ewan Gillespie has produced a work that will take you there too, to live his experiences and, for some of us, to re-live them. Set your compass now!

Neil Griffiths (author of *Hebridean Gurkha, Gurkha Highlander and Gurkha Reiver)*

Introduction

There can be no better way of exploring coastlines and coastal waters, mainland or island, than by sea kayak. Adept paddlers intent on reaching the 'inaccessible' need not be hindered by narrow inlets or protruding rocks. The kayak's hull draws just 2–3 inches of water which affords it great potential to delve into the unknown. Virtually silent, the craft can often approach marine life without causing distress. What does an otter or seal make of the strange shape approaching – a long hull with the top half of a human emerging from the middle, usually covered in great folds of Gortex and a silly hat? This evolutionary anonymity can have its problems, however, when 40-foot minke whales or a pod of dolphins draw close, sometimes within inches, to examine the nature of this rare marine inhabitant. What other sea-going vessel can land on rocks or shallow sandy bays in surf without incurring significant damage? What boat can meander through sea caves or be carried across land to the next point of entry to the sea?

Although no longer made from stitched animal hide, such as seal skin, modern sea kayaks are not far removed from their historic predecessors in sub-arctic regions of North America, Greenland and north-east Asia. Kayaks are now available in a wide variety of designs and materials. Driven by a desire to travel and explore in a manner that causes little damage to their surroundings, many coastal and wildlife explorers have taken to paddling.

My own sea background lay in two decades of scuba diving around Scotland. The sub-surface part of the sport was a tremendous thrill but long hours of travel in powered boats (required to transport divers and their heavy kit to a dive site), followed by only 20–30 minutes or so under water, eventually finished that sport for me. As so little time was spent diving I came to realise that it was the lure of the scenery and wilderness of the coast that drew me back again and again. The time had come to cast off my diving paraphernalia and look for a suitable sea-going vehicle to explore the west coast. Having paddled kayaks at school I knew a little of what was necessary. During a winter of training in the Ullapool swimming pool I mastered the Eskimo roll and various self-rescue techniques. I bought my first boat and cast off.

As the following pages will show, in our early ventures out to sea we were sometimes naïve and ill-prepared. Anyone taking up this pastime should ensure that they are fully trained both in their personal paddling and rescue skills. A good understanding of sea and weather changes are also essential.

The first step for our trips was to select an interesting stretch of coastline that would offer the chance to paddle for about a week. Normally, little detailed planning followed. Our aim was to leave the trip as open as possible to the whim of the group and the vagaries of the weather. As long as the holds were full of tasty food and some fine wine we were set for a good voyage. Some of the best days have not been spent in glorious sunshine on flat seas, but in howling storms inside the tents, playing 'Boggle' and drinking a good Aussie white.

This is not a book of esoteric expeditions to far flung corners of the world. All the routes described are possible for skilful kayakers with appropriate expertise, equipment and an abundance of enthusiasm. Extraordinary exploration of Scotland's magnificent west coast and islands can be yours.

I hope this book will inspire.

Ewan Gillespie

The author skirting the north of the Isle of Skye

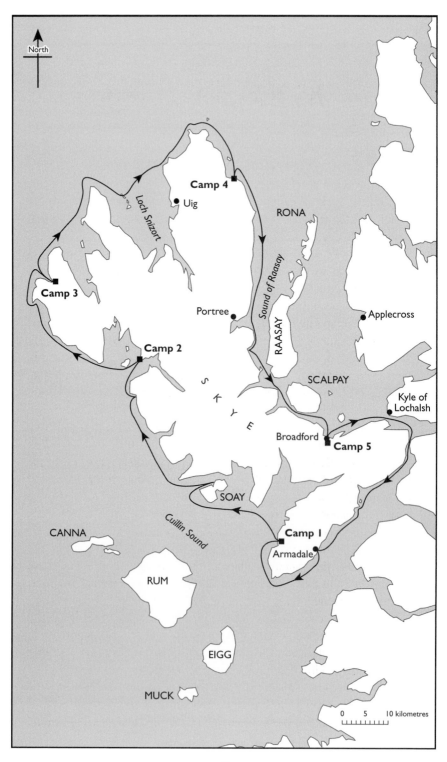

North

Camp 4

Uig

RONA

Loch Snizort

Camp 3

Sound of Raasay

Portree

Applecross

RAASAY

Camp 2

SCALPAY

Kyle of
Lochalsh

S K Y E

Broadford

Camp 5

SOAY

CANNA

Cuillin Sound

Camp 1

Armadale

RUM

EIGG

MUCK

0   5   10 kilometres

Chapter 1

Skye, just turn right

'Is this really a good idea?' I muttered to Mike as we drove out of the café car park at Invermoriston. The weather was practically the worst it could be with strong westerly winds buffeting the car and lashing the heavy rain sideways against us. Mike's wife, Bridget, had already called it a day and returned home to Perth. Not having an alternative plan we decided to persevere and see what conditions at Armadale, our starting point, would be like.

Mike had been planning this circumnavigation of Skye for some time and on a trip round Jura earlier in the year he mentioned to me that he was looking for companions for a two-week trip. With only one week off work I set off with Mike to see how far I could travel before cutting free at the end of the first week and thumbing a lift back to my car. Mike had arranged with other kayaking friends to join him for the second week to complete the circle of the island.

We had chosen September, the beginning of autumn, a month that often offers prolonged periods of calm weather but also heralds the first gales of a long Scottish winter. As we approached the watershed at the Cluanie Inn it did seem that the gales were already setting in; on either side of the glen swollen streams flooded down the hills in great ribbons of white, occasionally whisked into the air as updrafts caught the water tumbling from the numerous waterfalls.

We planned to set off from Armadale in the south west of Skye and circumnavigate the island in a clockwise direction. As the prevailing weather was from the south west the odds would be that should there be high winds and rough seas these would be on our backs when kayaking on the more exposed west side, giving us a helping push up to the northern end. Once at the top, we surmised that we could paddle down the east side in relative shelter. That apart, it seemed to me that islands should be paddled in a clockwise direction, not for any good reason other than that has a more natural feel to it. The run up the west side of Skye would certainly be exposed but if we managed to grab a window of good weather then we could crack this part in a two-day paddle which would almost certainly assure us of success for the rest of the trip. Doing it the other way around would involve a three-day paddle up the east side which would lead to disappointment should we then not make it down the west side if the weather turned too inclement.

As we approached Kyle of Lochalsh and the Skye Bridge, the cloud began to break a little and patches of blue sky appeared further west; it seemed as if the low pressure was passing over. An hour or so later, when we arrived at Armadale pier the rain had stopped and the roads were drying fast in the afternoon warmth. We left the boats and kit on the pier and arranged to leave the car at the nearby youth hostel, promising to stay there on our return. The young Australian warden was 'cool, man' over this request and said he would keep an eye on it for us. Mike also was eyeing up a rather nice looking bottle of malt in the pier shop which he promised to buy himself if the circumnavigation was successful.

In the late afternoon as we packed our boats we wondered if we should postpone our departure until the following day. The forecast wasn't too bad for the next few days but deep down there was an unspoken desire to get going. The last items were shoved into the holds and we launched. With a final glance back at the black-painted bird on the wall of the pier shop we turned right to pass below the ferry pier and make our run down to the Point of Sleat. The first leg to the bottom right-hand corner of Skye was only a 10-kilometre paddle which we quickly covered. This gave us an immediate psychological boost at having reached our first significant turning point to begin the western side of Skye. As the swell running in from the west was breaking heavily over the rocks at the point Mike chose to run round the corner quite close in to enjoy the sensation of the surging rise and fall of the sea.

I stood a little further offshore to take some pictures of Mike with the sea breaking on the rocky point behind him. The light was poor and the pictures were underexposed. In the course of the trip I regretfully took very few photographs of the stunning scenery, either because we were paddling too hard to stop or were setting up camp in order to settle, exhausted after each day's paddling.

By now the light was dimming rapidly in the early evening. We stopped at the little inlet of Acairseid an Rubha, just north of the Point of Sleat. In the shelter of the low hills behind the foreshore stood an isolated house surrounded by a thick, almost impenetrable stockade of trees, brambles and honeysuckle. We popped up to check that we could camp below the house. By luck the owners were in and by even more luck it turned out that they happened to be the parents of a good friend of Mike's. We were invited in and spent a very sociable evening with them. They lived here in this remote corner of Sleat during the summer months but had a camper van to spend the winter months off Skye and in the warmer climes of mainland Europe. Was this the perfect way to live? I was very impressed by their collection of local books. The one that caught my attention was *Hebridean Sharker* by Tex Geddes. I had long been trying to buy a copy of the book about this local character's involvement with Gavin Maxwell's basking shark fishing days after the Second World War but copies were like basking sharks – almost impossible to find. Later, when we made a move to leave and set our tents up we were offered the use of the floor in the main room where we settled down to a pleasant sleep in the warmth of the coal fire. In the flickering glow of the fire I read the first chapter of Tex's book and looked forward to stopping on Soay the next day, the island where Tex and Maxwell's shark fishery was based.

Next morning we were up early and off before our hosts rose. We had tied our boats to a fence at the top of the shoreline in case the weather turned through the night and washed them out to sea. Dawn was breaking to reveal a clear sky, and as the forecast had predicted, the winds were light southerlies making for ideal paddling conditions. Off to the north-east of us the jagged bulk of the Cuillins was catching the first light of the rising sun, glistening the wet slabs behind Loch Coruisk. In our little inlet the bushes were covered in a thick layer of morning dew and the chill feeling of autumn was definitely upon us. It took quite an effort to get going, but thanks to our kind hosts' hospitality we only had sleeping bags to pack into our boats.

The first 12 kilometres of paddling took us due north, running straight towards the southerly point of the Elgol peninsula before veering off as we approached the headland, then running west to the island of Soay. The sea was calm and the paddling easy. We decided to run into Soay from the north side, to the natural safe harbour where Gavin Maxwell had built his shark processing factory from the remains of the original herring plant. Now the building stood derelict, only used as a store for prawn creels and buoys.

On my first trip to Soay in 1998 I had sloped off work early one Friday afternoon and headed to Elgol to make the short paddle over to the south bay, arriving in the warmth of the late afternoon. Having set up my tent I had wandered through the dense birch woods across the narrow isthmus that joined the two halves of the dumb-bell-shaped island. The honeysuckle was in full bloom and the smell was unforgettable as I made my way to see the old shark factory. Later, with time in hand I wandered over to see the village. The scatter row of houses along the shore seemed empty but as I passed by a small tin-roofed house with a very neat garden a woman's voice called out, 'Are you Ewan?'

I was dumbfounded. How on earth did anyone there know me? Coming down to the garden gate she introduced herself as Jan Lovat, niece of Tex Geddes. Would I like to come in for a bite to eat? A mutual friend, Sanders Campbell, had phoned ahead to tell her to watch out for a lone kayaker. Jan and her husband, Ian, were retired and spent much of the summer on the island. Over the meal, our conversation turned to the shark fishery, Maxwell and Tex. Then came my second shock: Tex had died the previous week. After his funeral service he had been cremated and his ashes were now sitting above us on the kitchen mantlepiece waiting to be scattered on his beloved island the following day.

That night various islanders trickled in for a drink and a chance to tell a story or two about Tex. It was late when I made my slightly befuddled departure and staggered out into the dark of the night. One problem: I didn't know where my tent was as I had approached the village by a round about route earlier on. I was now more than a little lost. A couple of hours later I finally came across the tent having zigzagged over moor and bog. I crashed out just as the dawn light was breaking. After only a very short sleep a cuckoo sounded its morning call in a tree near my tent. This was the last straw. 'GO AWAY!' I hollered. It did, and I managed to sleep until lunchtime.

Later that day I explored more of the island, stopping at Tex's house below the rocky outcrop at the edge of the bay, the front door with its brass porthole giving the only visible hint of its colourful former owner, the laird of Soay. Tex Geddes who died while returning from a bagpiping competition in the Outer Hebrides was a character of near-heroic stature. Born in 1919, Joseph 'Tex' Geddes (he claimed he was given his nickname by a fellow commando of Red Indian origins) first became known to the wider world as Gavin Maxwell's harpoonist during the latter's ill-fated post-war attempt to establish a basking shark fishing industry in the Hebrides.

Gavin Maxwell went on to become a celebrated writer of books about natural history – notably *Ring of Bright Water* (1960) – but his first venture into print, following the collapse of his shark-fishing enterprise and an attempt at becoming a painter, was *Harpoon at a Venture* (1950) in which the central character was Geddes. The two had met at the Special Forces training camp in Arisaig on the West Coast in 1942 where they were both instructors. Maxwell, then aged twenty-eight, was an officer and an aristocrat, and taught field craft and small arms while twenty-four-year-old Geddes, a sergeant in the Seaforth Highlanders, specialised in amphibious warfare (explosives and boat handling). Geddes was an accomplished knife-thrower, bayonet fencer, a boxer, and a former rum-runner in Newfoundland. An orphaned lumberjack 'tree monkey' whose father had been blown up while dynamiting a log jam, he had been expelled from school at the age of twelve for being 'unmanageable'. By his own account, he was born in Peterhead and two years later was taken to Canada by his father following an altercation with the police. Others maintain he was the youngest of three fighting brothers and was raised by an aunt in Easter Ross, and never set foot in Canada. His neighbours, in nearby Skye, believed that he hailed from Australia. No matter. For Maxwell, Geddes was the personification of the 'man of action', and at the end of the war he employed him as his lieutenant when he bought Soay and set up his shark-fishing enterprise. The business was not a success, largely due to Maxwell's financial naïvety, and the company was in liquidation by 1952.

Geddes and his wife Jeanne bought Soay from the receiver. The other inhabitants of the island meanwhile requested evacuation, and Geddes was soon involved in a complex legal dispute over compensation for assets abandoned and improvements made to crofts. A long wrangle in the Scottish Land Court led to a change in the law, but Geddes had to sell part of the island in order to meet their obligations. The authorities were only persuaded to continue postal and telephone services when Geddes got his friends to send him numerous telegrams and registered packages (some of which contained only stones). Thirty years were to elapse before Geddes managed to buy back the part of the island he had sold. During this time he concentrated at first on writing his account of the shark-fishing adventure, *Hebridean Sharker* (1960). Later on he bred ponies and became involved with inshore fishing from his well-known boat, *Shearwater*, an activity which he romantically described as 'ploughing the fields between Scotland and America'.

Tex's last boat, *MV Petros,* still lies, rather forlornly, on a foreshore by the side of Loch Slapin on Skye.

For Mike and I there would be limited stopping places on the next part of the Skye coast. We made Soay an early lunch stop and sat on a small rocky promontory across from the old shark factory enjoying the warmth from the weak autumn sun. The rusty old steam boiler, salvaged from a steam engine that had powered the factory, caught the light and radiated an intense burnt umber colour. For my lunches I had bought a large number of tinned sardines: sardines in brine, sardines in sunflower oil, and sardines in tomato sauce. On this first full day of paddling I thought sardines on oatcakes a fine lunch; five days later I was sick of the sight of them. As there was little opportunity to buy alternative food I have been put off sardines in any shape or form for ever.

As the day was still young we decided to push on to Loch Bracadale to the north and set up camp there, giving us a relatively easy first full day of paddling. Mike and I had paddled once only together before, but as that was in a larger group we each weren't sure how far the other could travel in a day. Anyway, the weather was good and the forecast was promising for the following day. After lunch we set off northwards, round the headland before Glenbrittle, past Loch Eynort then pulled in for a comfort stop in Talisker Bay. On the beach a couple of families were playing with orange fishing buoys as we coasted in on the low surf. Oddly the Talisker distillery is on the other side of this land mass and sits on the shores of Loch Harport – perhaps the name '12 year old Harport' doesn't have the same cachet as '12 year old Talisker'.

Many years ago my boss and I were to undertake a dye dispersion study of the outfall pipe carrying the liquid waste from Talisker distillery. After a guided tour of the distillery and a couple of tasters of the product we were just about to pour the red dye down the outfall pipe when the manager asked if the deep red rodamine dye would stain oyster flesh. It would indeed! It turned out that there was an oyster farm quite near, which we didn't know about – a close call indeed for our agency's insurance and PR department (not to mention our jobs).

From Loch Brittle the cliffs of the west coast of Skye were spectacular, rising sheer out of the sea to 800 feet or so. We hugged the coast below them, enjoying the feeling of remoteness while starting to gel as a paddling team. Mike paddled at a speed that suited me perfectly and the weather was ideal, no waves and a gentle swell running in lazily from the west. By late afternoon we had turned into the wide expanse of Loch Bracadale and began the search for a good place to camp for the night. On the mainland side of the tidal causeway to the island of Oronsay we found a perfect spot at Ullanish Point.

The boats were easy to drag up the cobbled foreshore to a small flat grassy area. We set up the tents in the shelter of a rocky outcrop and a simple clothes line to air our already 'maturing' paddling attire. I've since paddled the length and breadth of Loch Bracadale many times and have not found a camping site that would better this one. Once fed, we walked up to the hotel at Ullinish Lodge but as it wasn't very welcoming, we made some phone calls and retreated to the tents.

We had covered 56 kilometres that day and had found that we worked well together. It was a contented pair of travellers who sat and listened to the news and weather on the radio that night. The forecast for the morrow predicted a small front passing to the south of us. Sleep was restless that night at the prospect of rounding Neist Point, which, in climbing terms, would be the crux move, the make or break part of the trip. Tidal streams running south on the ebb flow hit the point and deflect off to the west in a wide turbulent river. With any opposing wind this stream kicks up into a dangerous piece of water and we had heard several stories of hairy passages in fishing boats, never mind kayaks, round the headland.

We set off early, just after 7 a.m., my neck muscles stiff from the previous day's paddling. I still felt tired as we skirted the island of Wiay. A wonderful series of chasms and caves run deep into the cliffs on the north side. We poked our kayaks into a couple of them but this only elicited a deluge of cormorant pooh as the startled birds flapped past trying desperately to gain flying speed and height as they passed over us – jettisoning faecal weight seemed a valid and consistent way of achieving this.

Leaving Wiay behind, we crossed the open mouth of Bracadale. Back on the open sea we picked up a southerly swell running from behind us. The predicted bad weather to the south of us affected the sea around us. Our first 'way point' of the morning was Idrigill Point and the MacLeod's Maidens lying just off it. These are a set of three sea stacks sitting under the high cliffs of the point that are prone to catching both the tidal currents and the effects of any downdraft from the sheer cliffs above. We steered a course between the first and second of the maidens, hoping they would be kind to us. This was a bad choice. Although the swell wasn't big, somehow it seemed to get itself wedged under the skirts of the maidens and the combined effects of this funnelling and the resultant clapotis produced an area of chaotic, crashing waves caught between the rock towers with nowhere to escape. We should have backed out at the first sign of this pandemonium but didn't. Although the passage was only a couple of hundred metres, it was daunting. Waves were bouncing back and fore towards us, looking like little jagged alpine peaks, calling for frantic bracing strokes on alternating sides of the boat as one after the other the peaks clattered into our sides, almost slowing our forward progress to a complete halt. The boats rose and fell amazingly quickly in this ragged sea – it was very disturbing to the senses, and stomach. The ten minutes of extreme effort required to pass through this area left us drained. At the other side of this mayhem we rafted up to catch our breath.

'I wasn't happy in that.' Mike said quietly as we drank from our hydration tubes to wet our dry throats. It's odd that what scares one person doesn't always scare another. I didn't like the frantic energy of the jumble of waves but felt safe enough. What was to come later that day, however, put the fear of God into me but did not seem to faze Mike nearly as much.

A series of clefts and caves on the next section of cliff was breathtaking. One in particular, at the start of Moonen Bay, had a waterfall running off its apex. We took it in turns to paddle beneath it, allowing our salty kit to get thoroughly rinsed in the fine spray of freshwater. It was cold but pleasantly invigorating. This area around Moonen Bay was a well-known gathering place for basking sharks and one of Maxwell and Geddes' top hunting zones. The high energy of the currents in the area produced a wealth of feeding for the large fish. As we paddled closer to Neist the sea state increased from the south and the sky was becoming rather dark above us. A rising following sea sometimes catches out the unwary. Initially it proves helpful with forward progress, but then the paddler realises the waves are far too big for comfort and the power of the sea can be immense.

I well remember a friend and I being caught in a force 7 storm on a trip back from the Isle of Eigg to the mainland at Arisaig. We had obtained a weather forecast from a yacht anchored in Galmisdale after our rough crossing from Muck: a storm was imminent. We took the chance that we could be on the Arisaig side before it hit us. At about a third of the way across the seas became too big to turn back. We plunged on. Half way over, two fishing trawlers passed in front of us. We back-paddled to check our forward motion to let them past. Detached, I sat there amazed by the frantic motion of the boats as they pitched and rolled violently, rising and falling into the wave troughs with spectacular crashes. For a few seconds one of the boats slowed slightly and someone came out of the wheelhouse to give us an enquiring wave. We couldn't wave back as our hands were too tightly gripped to the paddle shafts. I tried to smile and pretend that we were having a jolly fine crossing – not that the fishing boats could have assisted anyway.

My overriding memory of that trip was the tremendous sound of the breaking wave crests over our heads and the green water that I could see along the face of the waves as they bore my kayak sideways along each of them. The wave breaks would dump a good weight of water onto the topsides of the kayak, after deluging down the neck of my cagoule, and in the occasional mega one, the boat would vanish beneath me, leaving me sitting there, a half-person in the ocean holding a paddle, before rising again. I was scared. My paddling partner's boat didn't have the luxury of a skeg. He had to make steering-correction-strokes constantly to keep his boat pointing east towards Arisaig, and safety, whereas I set my skeg to keep the boat on course across the beam sea. A couple of hours later we arrived at the reefs at the entrance to Loch nan Ceall which leads into the village of Arisaig. Trying to time our entrance through the crashing sea to avoid being trashed on the rocks took an age. Although I'm not a smoker I was very happy to have a few deep drags on Tim's slightly soggy roll-up when we made it through to shelter.

Now, on Skye, with the seas becoming bigger, the closer we got to Neist, the more we were losing our, by now, fairly efficient paddling progress. Part of the reason for our early start was to allow us a window of opportunity to pass Neist Point at high water slack tide. Despite the following seas we made progress northwards more slowly than expected. We were now behind schedule and as we drew up under the shelter of the bay south of the Neist lighthouse, we knew that we had missed our slot in the tide. Although the tide had only been on the ebb for an hour at the most, the water flow was streaming southwards at a brisk rate and meeting the northbound swell head on, producing some spectacular lumps and sliding seas. To cap it all, the rain began. We were weary and I had to remind myself that this was a holiday. It became quickly obvious that we should not attempt the passage round the point in these conditions. Our only option was to pull up on the foreshore near to the lighthouse jetty for a snack and a planning session.

We were cold, tired, hungry and more than a little dejected as we stood in the pouring rain, the only souls about in this usually busy tourist part of Skye. Mike then produced a lifesaver, a rip-stop nylon, two-person shelter. We grabbed some food from the holds and squatted under the welcome shelter on the sodden grass. The difference inside this thin-walled cover was staggering. Out of the wind and rain we became warm in minutes and ate our food in relative comfort. Even better, the nylon was a nice yellow-orange colour, enabling us to imagine that we were somewhere tropical. Yip! We really were on our holidays! We sat facing each other, knees jammed against knees, and so by the action of both of us leaning back against the nylon we could make the shelter quite stable. For a long period we dozed, happy in the now warm, steaming microclimate that we had combined to make. I could have stopped here easily for the day but we needed to get past the crux and push on for the remainder of the day.

After several half-hearted attempts we emerged from the shelter back into the cold wind and rain to walk over the cliff tops above the point to check out the sea below. The sea was vicious and still streaming southwards with a tremendous force. By lying flat on the cliff top and peering directly down to the water a hundred feet below us we studied the eddies and backwaters just by the base of the cliff. We could just make out little areas of quieter water which we thought we could possibly use to hop from one patch to another in safety if we paddled hard. I was getting cold again and was keen to try something – anything to get warm. We decided to go for it.

Back on the water, Mike, skilled in white-water paddling, went first. At the south end of the Point we sat in a spot of relatively calm water and carefully lined up the boats, facing north and parallel to the cliffs above, before giving a quick sideways motion with the paddle to push the boat into the oncoming torrent. We then paddled like fury to gain the first back eddy and safety. I let Mike do this eddy hop twice to allow me a degree of flexibility to slot into a haven which he then vacated for the next. This was more than a bit hair-raising and I was not a happy bunny. To our left the hard-running southerly ebb flow driving into the oncoming swell produced ferocious standing waves that rose and dipped in 5-foot crashes. To my immediate right the cliffs rose vertically above so that each scrabble to the next quiet water area meant that my paddle blade clattered against rock as I sought some sort of purchase on rock or water to drive my boat forward. Half way along the Point we stopped in a dark cleft in the cliff from which we could look up and see the lighthouse's trumpet-shaped foghorn above our heads, and also the septic tank outfall pipe. Please let the building be empty, I pleaded to myself. To be deluged in crap would be the final ignominy of the day.

Another 20 minutes of this scrabbling and we were out of the worst of the current. For the next part of the coast we were in more exposed water but with a constant current that was moving more slowly south. Although progress was slow, we eventually left Oisgill Bay behind and turned into Loch Pooltiel and our finishing point for the day. The tide was getting low by late afternoon and we had a long portage up the beach to our new campsite situated safely up on the grassy verges of the road to the small hamlet of Glendale. The only flat patch of land was an area where the local fish farmer had left a salmon cage plastic flotation ring. That was good enough for us. We set up the tents inside the circle, using the walkway stanchions as anchor points for our guy lines. I recall vaguely that there was a blood-red sunset that night but after that I was lost to the land of nod and a deep sleep.

All too soon my watch beeped: 5.30 a.m. and time to turn the radio on for the shipping forecast. I secretly wished for a storm forecast so that we could take the day off and have a rest. My neck muscles were still giving me jip and I was not in the most enthusiastic of moods to take to the water again. We were to start our run along the north of the island and that involved the three big headlands of Dunvegan, Waternish and Rubha Hunish; the latter would have a fairly brisk tidal flow for us to overcome if we timed it badly.

Dunvegan Head heralded the end of the west coast and was the second corner of the four that were required for success. The 8 kilometres to the turn were achieved in an easy sea, but the wind had changed through the night and was now coming from the west. My neck and shoulders were as stiff as boards and even trying to flex them before setting off gave me shooting needles of pain. It was a relief to get to the turn at the headland and point the boats north-east to line up with the distant grey headland of Waternish Point 10 kilometres away, although in the gloom of the early morning it seemed more like forty. At the turn I welcomed the assistance with our forward motion that the following sea provided and I could ease a little the strain on my aching upper body. It was not yet 8 a.m. when we cleared, in good fettle, the first of the big three northerly headlands of Skye. The straight-line paddle to Waternish was unremarkable and quick as we settled into a routine of paddling and sporadic but easy chat, chewing over our lives and future plans. Mike's ambition was to set up a campsite somewhere on the west coast and spend the winters skiing and mountaineering abroad.

Ambling across the opening of Loch Dunvegan we initially failed to notice that the morning flood tide was pushing us slightly to the south into the loch itself. That didn't really matter as we steered a little further north to compensate. Half way across we could see the low-lying island of Isay, owned in fairly recent times by the folk singer Donovan. Its owner of 400 years earlier, Roderick MacLeod of Lewis, was less benign and, if the tales are true, a nasty character. But for two families who were next in line to inherit the island of Raasay and also the lands of Gairloch, MacLeod's grandson could stake his claim to these sought-after islands. The cunning MacLeod invited both families to a great banquet at his house on Isay. As the night progressed he sought the private view of each family member on a matter of great importance. One by one, as the guests entered the private chamber off the hall, Roderick had them stabbed to death.

Our next target, Waternish Point, was a low lying promontory. It was difficult to gauge its size as, even from a couple of kilometres or so away, it still looked a long way off. Reaching it sooner than we expected was consequently very satisfying. From the turn at Waternish we couldn't even see the final headland at Rubha Hunish which lay deep in the gloom over 20 kilometres away, still to the north-east. As we needed a short break we turned into Loch Snizort and aimed for the Ascrib Islands, 5 kilometres to our right. A strong counter current from the west side of Snizort made for a hard paddle to our landing on the biggest island of South Ascrib. Unlike at the previous island, Isay, there was no need to fear the ghosts of a long ago slaughter but we did look out, without success, for a subterranean house built somewhere here in 1985 by the owner at the time.

We sat eating (yes, more sardines) as we listened to the lunchtime shipping forecast, which predicted force 8 southerlies for the next day. This didn't sound so good; we packed up and pushed on to cross Loch Snizort to get round our final headland as quickly as we could, just in case the gales came in faster than predicted. It is usually worth pushing the pace in such circumstances to 'get round the next headland' as this can make or break a trip.

As we left the shelter of the Ascribs the sea and winds picked up and an hour or so later we had a steady force 4–5 on our backs. This made for very quick forward progress and relief for our tired bodies. We were riding quickly through waves of 4 feet in height, constant bracing and rudder strokes keeping us on course. Immersed in our energetic activity we didn't notice the Lochmaddy to Uig ferry bearing down on us from the left. As it loomed into view we knew that we wouldn't be spotted easily in the waves. By veering sharp left towards the oncoming vessel we slowed our forward momentum and allowed our boats to broach westwards across the waves. We let the ferry slide past our right-hand sides some 100 metres away, before turning in behind it to cut straight across its wake.

We resumed our passage to Rubha Hunish, aiming slightly off to the south to head for the far side of the loch near Tulm Island. An hour or so later and 6 kilometres further across the loch we could see the returning ferry leaving Uig Bay and setting its course back over the Minch. Ha, we thought smugly, it will pass way behind us. But no! Its return route was more to the north-west as it took a triangular route and headed for Tarbert on Harris. As it dawned on us that it was trying to 'take us out' a second time, we didn't hang about and paddled like fury to cut across its track to safety. I would love to find out from a CalMac skipper whether kayaks can be seen in the water, and if they can, would the ferries deviate from their set course to miss them. I have a warped image of a series of notches cut into the ferry steering wheel signifying the wipe out of kayaks. Hopefully there weren't too many 'Aces' in the fleet.

After the long crossing we finally pulled into the lee of Tulm Island, a long upturned boat-hulled shape of a rock, but one that provided shelter for a much needed rest. It was now late in the afternoon and we were approaching the most northerly point on Skye. Rubha Hunish lay only 3 kilometres further on. We were tired but eager to push on and round the top of the island before calling it a day. The sea state was still brisk and we had no idea how bad the tidal stream would be around the headland. Our calculations for the day didn't include this last headland nor the effects that the westerly sea would have. What the heck! We decided to try it and pulled out of the shelter of Tulm and began again, chopping and bracing hard in the beam sea on our left hand side. Rounding the first headland we slid along under the high cliffs, which to our pleasant surprise, gave immediate shelter from the wind and, more importantly, the oncoming sea. Within a few metres we were paddling in calm water, albeit with frequent, sudden downdrafts scudding past us across the indented north coast. Two kilometres to our left lay the small islet of Eilean Trodday but we weren't tempted to round it as the tidal race could be seen running offshore some 200 metres out from where we were paddling. The sea cliffs here were stunning and we slowed right down to potter in amongst the clefts and caves.

We were now paddling due east and after half an hour or so we ran out of cliff as the coast turned sharply to our right and dropped away south. The third corner of Skye! Two in one day! Even better, we were still inside the track of the tidal rip and missing it entirely. Our map showed a small inlet 3 kilometres to the south at Kilmaluag Bay. With renewed energy we paddled down to make this our stop for the night, well pleased with our day's progress. We both had a growing feeling that we had the trip cracked and success was within grasp. This intrigued me. It was now Tuesday; we had paddled roughly half way round the island. I had another three or four days left before I had to head home and I began to realise that I too could finish the paddle and complete the entire circumnavigation of Skye.

There was no way ashore on the kelp-covered steep rocks that ringed the far end of the bay between the cliffs on either side. We searched for a good twenty minutes or more but to no avail. We did not wish to risk wrecking our boats carrying them over the slippery rocks. Checking the map, we could see that it would be a good 8 kilometres further down the coast before we could make another attempt to go ashore at Staffin Bay. There was no choice. A little dejectedly we pushed on.

The spectacular cliffs with deep dark arches and high stacks kept our minds off tired muscles. I discussed my earlier musings with Mike. If he had other friends joining him later in the week he could stop for a few days of rest before completing the journey. I would be happy to plough on to circuit the island back to Armadale alone. As I was familiar with most of the coast from Portree down through Kylerhea and back to our starting point I felt confident doing a solo passage. To my pleasant surprise, Mike said that he too had been mulling over the options for the remaining part of the trip. He was keen to push on with me. We had paddled well together and both of us were prepared to begin early and make good progress on the water to achieve reasonable mileages each day. Furthermore, the forecast was looking more unsettled and the weather might close in for the season.

With a tacit understanding we completed our last few kilometres into Staffin Bay. To our right the sun was setting over the jagged outline of the Quiraing on the Trotternish ridge. The dimming light projected displays of pinks, reds and browns on the cloud above. It was sheltered and seemingly settled here but with the force 8 forecast we were glad to be finishing for the day. We thought we could at least get a shower at the campsite up the hill above Staffin on the following day. I was pretty washed out when we finally arrived on the wet, flat foreshore. The tide was out and the portage of the boats and kit to our grassy camping spot was slow. We had found a neat little dip in the back of the sand dunes out of view of the houses of the nearby village which we hoped would offer shelter from strong winds forecast for the following day. Despite having to carry the boats up to the camp we were both elated and a little light-headed from exhaustion and hunger, but mainly because it had been one of the best day's paddling ever. The scenery was superb and we had safely paddled the entire north side of the island in one fell swoop. Later that evening Mike calculated that we had covered 65 kilometres: a distance well and truly felt in my neck and shoulder muscles.

We agreed that, regardless of weather, the next day would be a rest day. The alarm on my watch was turned off and I planned to sleep in as long as I could. This I eventually accomplished, but only after getting up through the night to re-peg the tent's guy lines. The storm had duly arrived in the darkness and howled over our heads. I could hear the waves crashing onto the foreshore in the bay below us. Content in the warmth of my sleeping bag, I enjoyed the feeling of security inside the wind-lashed tent, glad to be here rather than out at sea.

Wednesday was a delight. A lazy 8 o'clock start, lots of coffee and Trangia-mottled toast, then a quick trip to the nearest house to refill our water sacks. Naïvely, we wandered up the hill to the campsite to ask if we could pay for a shower. The old grump at reception told us to go away as we weren't residents. We explained that we couldn't have got our gear up to the site and that we would happily pay whatever he wanted for a wash – no dice. Scottish inhospitality still prevailed apparently. He could, without bother, have charged us a pound or so for a shower. At the very least, it would have engendered some good will. Instead, we told our friends never to go there. I resorted to an awkward strip wash in the vestibule of my tent, ducking low to avoid being spotted by local residents in the nearby house over the field. The rest of the day was spent snoozing, drinking coffee, reading, and in the afternoon, a leisurely stroll up the Quiraing.

We were lucky to have picked such a sheltered spot as we could see the the sea being kicked into a ferocious turmoil by gale force winds. Just out from Staffin Bay lay the small island of Eilean Flodigarry. I lay in the long marram grass on top of the dunes watching the waves break high onto the rocks at the south end of the island. The explosions must have risen over a hundred feet into the air. I tried to capture this on film but the prints failed to capture the beauty and scale of the spectacle.

Our meal that evening was a long-drawn-out affair. I remember spooning out half peaches from a ragged-edged can; they tasted wonderful, washed down with an overpriced bottle of red wine from the local shop. We sat in the gloaming pouring over the South Skye map, working out various permutations of the route for the next two days. Raasay lay across the channel and was always an enjoyable place to paddle past. Alternatively, we could pass between the south end of Raasay and Scalpay, then hop to Kyle via the series of islands of Longay and Pabay. These were the more exposed routes, but with the poor weather expected, we decided to play it safe and keep tight against the coast of Skye for maximum shelter from the elements. Our route for the next day would be 30 kilometres due south, stopping overnight at a friend's house at Camus Tianavaig, a few kilometres down the coast from Portree.

Morning crept in all too soon. In the dark, after our day off, it took quite a mental effort to rise from my warm sleeping bag to resume paddling again especially as I was still tired (and my head suffering from red wineitis). It was still blowy when we left the shelter of the bay and when we turned right the wind was head on to us. The sea had dropped overnight but was still a good force 4 and paddling was tiring. Progress was slow as we picked our way south, high cliffs once more towering above us. When we came to the tourist view point at the so-called Kilt Rock a bus load of visitors was being disgorged for the inevitable photo opportunity. One person waved down to us before dashing back on to the bus – perhaps to be whisked off to a warm coffee shop. This gave rise to a long fantasy conversation about skinny lattes and wonderful cream cakes. Somehow the diet of pasta and sardines had lost its appeal and we made up our minds to stop at Portree to buy the biggest, most sickly cake that we could find.

Sometime later we reached Rubha nam Brathairean, a small promontory in the otherwise straight coast. Sheltered by rocks we rested for a few minutes and drank some water. As we sat chatting, two more sea kayakers appeared round the little headland and pulled in beside us. They were a couple from North Wales doing the same trip as us but the other way around! A long-range weather forecast, they said, predicted gales approaching in two days time. As we swapped experiences it transpired that they had been at this undertaking for the last ten days! They seemed a little lost as to what they should do: to go on and brave the northern and west side or to pack it all in and return another year. We pointed out on the map some of the good places to camp and various places where tides called for great care before wishing them well. What they decided to do, we never did find out. They told us of two occasions when they were coming to fairly significant headlands towards the end of the day and how they had stopped short to set up camp so that they would be rested for the following day. On both occasions the weather had turned nasty overnight preventing them from moving on. Getting round headlands if at all possible now seemed wiser than ever.

We slogged on down the coast for another 16 kilometres to the opening into Loch Portree. By now it was raining hard and our spirits were low. We looked towards the town which seemed very grey through the curtain of rain. Our earlier thoughts of sticky cakes were forgotten; all we wanted was to stop paddling and get warmed up. Camus Tianavaig was less than an hour's paddle away. We would slog on to finish our journey there. At least there would be a warm shower and a chance to get the kit dried out.

Just south of Portree we passed a sea eagle, sitting hunched on a large rock by the water's edge. We slowed as we passed by. It swivelled its head to watch but that apart it didn't move a muscle. It looked as cheesed off with the weather as we were. These magnificent birds can be seen regularly in this part of Skye, following the relative success of their re-introduction using birds from northern Norway. I had once spent a winter on a ski touring holiday north of Tromsö, in the Lyngen Alps area, and as we drove to the hills each day from our camp on the coast, the sea eagle was the bird most frequently seen. Its immense size was hard to believe. One of my skiing companions thought 'it was like a pair of flying ironing boards.' I wondered what they ate. 'Probably anything they damn-well like …' was the response. These great birds once inhabited the entire coastline of Britain. Persecuted by man, their main predator, they survived a little longer than elsewhere on Scotland's west coast because of its remoteness and craggy coastline.

It was well past lunchtime when we pulled up below Becky's house in Tianavaig Bay. The low red tin-roofed croft house was set tight against the hill behind; an old bus was abandoned to one side and acted as a store house. Just where we went ashore a large upturned wooden dingy lay rotting in the front garden. Becky who worked in Portree had said she would leave us a key. We searched high and low but with no luck. Mike's mobile phone had no reception. We were a little flummoxed. What should we do? In the never-ending rain we crawled under the upturned dingy to have lunch. It was a bit cramped but at least we were out of the rain as we recharged our batteries on German rye bread and – yes, you guessed it: tinned small fish in tomato sauce. I tried to cheer us both up by relating a tale of Mark, a paddling friend, who was digging his boat out of the garage for his first trip of the year. When he removed the back hatch cover, to air the hold, he found a dead mouse lying inside. How it had got there puzzled him as the hold was sealed shut. What made us laugh was that next to the mouse was a loaf of dry, long-life rye bread, still in its cellophane wrapper, totally untouched by mouse tooth marks. Somehow this poor unfortunate creature had become incarcerated in Mark's back hold along with this forgotten loaf and had opted to die of starvation rather than postpone its demise by eating the rye bread. He buried the mouse under a large flat stone giving it a fitting eulogy for such a proud strong-minded act of culinary defiance.

Crouched under the dingy, the thought of waiting for another three hours for Becky to return from work was too much for us. It was only another 22 kilometres down the coast to Broadford. With much groaning, we crept from our cover like two hunched old men. Reluctantly, we headed back into the rain once more to resume the passage south.

I was a little out of it that afternoon. The cumulative effect of many days' strenuous activity was getting the better of me. I felt detached from events; the rain seemed to be falling on someone else, not on me. Not even the sight of two otters near the Raasay Narrows could pull me back from my remoteness.

Those last kilometres into Broadford are blank. Mike saw two more otters as we negotiated the shallows between Skye and Scalpay but I missed them. The last hour before our landing below the hostel was at least wind-free. The hills to our right provided shelter; the rain still fell but not sideways into my jacket hood and down my neck. In my kayak cockpit I was sitting in a pool of water that squelched around each time

I readjusted my aching beam end – the misery of the day was becoming too much to bear. I was so glad to feel the crunch of the bow as we landed on the gravel shore next to the Broadford pier. We made a final, it felt heroic, effort to carry the boats up to the grass lawn by the hostel and then stumbled, dripping, inside to book in for the night.

We had been paddling for the best part of eleven hours. Thankfully, because it was late in the season, the hostel was quiet. We spread out all our kayaking and camping gear in the drying room. I was soaked through and decided to strip off there and then, hanging every bit of soggy clothing up on a washing line. In an effort to retain some dignity and not get chucked out of the hostel, I re-donned my damp clingy nylon over trousers and made a dash for the shower room. This luxury was well overdue. I stayed under the steaming spray for as long as I could; warmth was slow to return but it was heaven. When I eventually emerged from the steam-laden cubicle I realised to my horror that I had not brought a towel nor dry clothes! I made one mad dash out of the hostel, back into the rain to the kayak, in my over-trousers, to find something to wear.

Later that evening, Mike called his friends to let them know of our progress and plans. They had been watching weather forecasts predicting steadily worsening conditions and had decided that the second week's paddling would not be on. They were also a bit surprised to find that we planned to complete our trip around Skye the following day.

We paddled out of Broadford Bay the next morning. I had fully recovered and was looking forward to the day's paddle down to Armadale. Taking a direct course from the pier towards the Skye Bridge, we crossed the mouth of Broadford Bay and within the first ten minutes or so we were passed by a small pod of four or five porpoises. To encounter a school of them was unusual as these are normally solitary creatures. We were indeed privileged to share, briefly, a small patch of grey sea with them.

Overnight the wind had dropped a little but it was till gusty as we passed by the small island of Pabay. Our progress towards Kyleakin was good as our chat turned to what would be next on our paddling itinerary. My thoughts were of Norway and a trip from Stavanger to Bergen. Mike had already been and raved about the beauty of the coastline north of Haugesund and the fjords further north near Bergen. Our chat was short lived; within an hour or so the wind stiffened again and, of course, it blew straight towards us. Forward progress slowed right down. We perhaps had been too cocky coming up the west side of Skye with comparative ease. The elements were now out to remind us that it was they, not us, who were in charge here. The 'easy' east side had been a real slog all the way down from Rubha Hunish and even now as we approached the Skye Bridge, the weather was not going to let us off, even for one day. Passing under the bridge offered a real psychological boost and our spirits rose. We were almost at our fourth and last corner. I can't recall what the tide was doing as we slid past the island of Eilean Bhàn, the white island, the final home of Gavin Maxwell, now relegated to a stepping off point for the soaring bridge to Skye. Would he have smiled wryly over the madness of the funding and tolls' fiasco that has accompanied this crossing?

We were now on the last leg of the trip as we left the village of Kyleakin quickly behind. We crossed the small opening of Loch na Beiste, then the most easterly part of Skye before finally turning south and round our fourth corner to enter the Kylerhea narrows. Just before the turn we paddled over the mangled surface-protruding ironworks of the wreck of the *MV Port Napier*. During the Second World War the ships of the Port Line were commandeered to serve in the war effort. The *Napier* was converted to a mine laying ship and was taking on its cargo of 550 mines from the railhead at Kyle. For days the crew had laboured hard to stow away the dangerous cargo along narrow-gauge rails to the holds below. As the loading was almost complete a fire was spotted which quickly spread out of control. If the cargo had exploded, the village of Kyle would have been flattened in the blast. Consequently, the ship was cut free and towed to the other side of the channel where the burning vessel was cast free. Shortly afterwards it exploded, sending its bridge superstructure skywards several hundred feet to land on the shore of Skye where it sits today. The hull rapidly flooded with water and settled on its starboard side in 20 metres of water, with most of its mines still intact. There it sat for several decades until amateur divers began to explore it in the seventies. The navy became concerned and then made a concerted effort to remove the remaining ordnance as best they could.

I dived this wreck many times and was always wary when penetrating it down through the stern mine-laying tube as no-one was sure just how many mines had actually gone off or had been removed, and how many were still on board. We dived on the wreck to commemorate the 50th anniversary of its sinking. I remember dropping down to the seabed at the stern, a part I had never really dived before. Just where the curve of the stern met the sea bed I came across a brass porthole still attached to the hull. This must have been the last one left on this heavily-dived wreck. As I couldn't remove it with my dive knife I managed to persuade my diving friends to return two weeks later.

Laden with tools I descended to the same part of the wreck, only to find a dark hole in the rusty steel hull which had held my nice porthole. I couldn't believe it; it had been there for fifty years and I had missed getting it by less than two weeks.

The narrows of Kylerhea offered the final excitement of the trip. In this narrow channel the tides are squeezed through the gap between Skye and the mainland at speeds in excess of 12 knots. My first trip through here had been a solo effort as I paddled from Loch Carron, to the north, to Arnisdale in Loch Hourn, further to the south. I had timed my passage to coincide with mid-ebb, which heads south into the Sound of Sleat. I was in good form as I slid through the channel, carried by the current. I had back-paddled a little at Kylerhea itself to allow the small car ferry to pass in front of me before realising that I was in mid channel heading straight for a large tidal overfall. The next twenty minutes had been horrendous as eddies and boils rose up below me, sending my kayak skidding sideways, only to stop dead against the edge of the next eddy-line. I had worked hard and by the time I had passed on through and arrived at the Sandaig Islands (by the Camusfearna of Maxwell's *Ring of Bright Water* fame) I was emotionally and physically wiped out. I camped and slept on the main grassy part of the biggest island.

The following morning I was woken by the sound of two boats pulling up on the sandy beach nearby. Looking out of my tent I could see lots of people – at least four adults and seven or more small children clambering out of the dinghies. I slipped back in to my sleeping bag to finish my well-earned lie-in, but not for long. The two families had set up stumps for cricket wickets on the grass fairway where my tent lay mid way, and began to play. How surreal! I eventually emerged from my tent, taking care to avoid young Gus's poorly-aimed googlies as they skimmed off my outer tent fabric. This was too much for me, especially as they seemed to be totally oblivious to my presence bang in the middle of the wicket. Twenty minutes later as I finally packed my kayak and was about to launch one of the women stated casually, 'I hope we're not chasing you away?' What can you say to that?

As Mike and I turned south to paddle the last leg of the journey we didn't expect the east wind that had been in our faces all morning to then veer south too and to blow at us from up the narrows as we headed down towards the Sound of Sleat. This was really too much and it seemed as though the island was out to extract its pound of flesh from us and make us work hard for every metre gained. Fortunately, the tidal streams posed no real danger to us as the current through the narrows hadn't yet picked up its usual head of steam. We kept to the Skye shore until we were through the narrows then after a short stop we set into our final paddle back to our starting point at Armadale. The wind was still coming out of the south making the paddling hard work. We could now see the Island of Eigg in the far distance. Only 20 kilometres to go! Coming past the tidal island of Ornsay, Mike suddenly let out a sharp cry. In the effort to paddle forward he had torn a muscle in his shoulder. Each paddle stroke now produced a penetrating pain. We slowed right down to ease the pressure on his injury. Forward speed was now barely perceptible but Mike insisted he would make it. At last we saw the ferry pier at our journey's end at Armadale, and then the black painted bird on the shop – the finish. To complete the circumnavigation we made a short detour to pass 'over' our outbound track past the pier. We slipped into the shelter of the bay just as light was fading and sat offshore awhile savouring the moment. Strangely, we were both reluctant to finish and to touch the shore as it signalled the end of the trip. Out past the ferry slip in the Sound of Sleat the wind was picking up and the sea state was rising.

Later that evening, packed and showered, we sat in Ardvasar Hotel enjoying a celebratory pint or two of Guinness and a meal – not pasta, sardines or oatcakes. A very contented couple of paddlers staggered back to the hostel that night.

In the morning, we packed the car and headed for home. The weather had now 'lost the plot' and gale force winds were blowing the first autumnal-coloured leaves off the trees around the hostel. From the roadside by the shore we could just make out the Mallaig ferry crossing the Sound of Sleat through the gloom, crashing up and down in the big seas. Certainly paddling would have been impossible that day. We had been very lucky. We had just managed to complete the circuit before the weather closed it all down for another year.

Best meal on trip: sweet and sour vegetables

1 sliced onion
1 garlic clove, sliced
1 pepper, thinly sliced
1 carrot, thinly sliced
15-20 mushrooms, chopped or sliced
1 small tin of sweet corn
1 sachet of sweet and sour sauce, or similar
1 cupful of basmati rice

Fry the onion, pepper, garlic and carrots until soft, add the mushrooms and fry for another 2-3 minutes. Add the sweet corn and sauce mix. Simmer for 5 minutes. Remove from heat and set to one side. Place the rice in a pan and add water (twice the volume of rice). Simmer and cook.

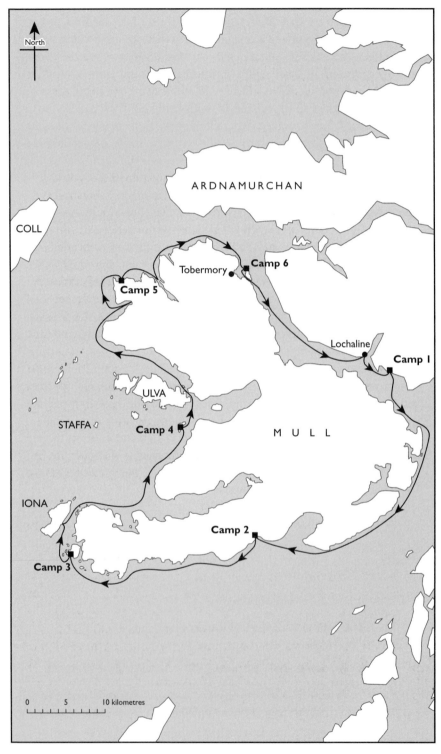

Chapter 2

Mull, all the way round

With the success of the Skye circumnavigation still fresh in my mind, I was eager to undertake other island trips of a similar ilk. This was not the beginning of some perverse form of island bagging. At this stage I had been hill walking for over twenty years and had only managed to 'bag' fewer than half of the Munros. Ticking items on a list wasn't important to me for either hills or seas. I enjoyed both for what they were. Looking back at my trip with Mike I appreciated that the thrill of Skye had been an amalgam of many different experiences and emotions. Inevitably, there had been the urgency to complete the journey before the autumn storms set in, and we had just made it by a matter of hours. For the whole week we had paddled with the ever-changing scenery of Skye in full view; scenery that rates as some of the best anywhere in the world. I suppose that, for me at least, the greatest exhilaration came from the physical demands of the trip and the paddling skills required to match the constantly changing moods of the currents, waves and wind.

The following winter I had poured over maps looking for further suitable island circumnavigations and Mull was proving to be a strong contender. The island was far less indented with sea lochs than Skye, which meant that a larger proportion of the coastline could be paddled without resort to crossing sea lochs from headland to headland when time was limited. Andrew Dempster, whose book, *Skye 360: Walking the Coastline of Skye (Luath Press 2003),* describes a long walk round the entire Skye coastline, calculated that the coast length was some 1,000 kilometres. It had taken us 306 kilometres to circle the island, which amounted to less that a third of the total. As the coast round Mull is approximately 400 kilometres and our trip was projected to cover 200 kilometres, the distance covered would therefore amount to a more healthy half of the total coastline.

One day in early spring, whilst flicking through the Scottish Canoe Association tour list for the year, I noticed an entry advertising that Joe Donaldson was organising a Mull expedition. This appealed to me as the hard graft of all necessary logistics would already have been undertaken. Although the tides around the island, with the exception of the Sound of Mull, weren't too much of a problem, the exposure on the south, west and northerly tip could cause many days of delay if the weather were to close in. A quick phone call later to Joe had it all sorted. As it happened, he had had little interest from the sea kayaking community and was on the verge of abandoning his plans as only one other person had shown interest. My phone call, offering the chance of two more persons in the group, swung it for Joe and the trip was definitely on.

There were four of us: Joe, Andrea, Wendy and myself. Joe was an amazing character who hailed from Penicuik, just south of Edinburgh. He was a businessman who at that time imported and sold cane furniture but had tried numerous disparate ventures over the years, including importing engines to power hang-gliders. He was in his late forties, of stocky build and grey beard. He reminded me very much of David Bellamy. Joe's great strengths were that he was always cheery and upbeat and of a very generous nature. As we were to learn through the trip, Joe did things Joe's way. This you had to accept, and despite occasional frustration it was impossible to get annoyed at him – a great paddling companion indeed.

Wendy hailed originally from New Zealand but now worked in Skye turning her hand to a variety of outdoor activities. She was very capable and her strong paddling skills were a real asset to the group. Coincidentally, Wendy was a friend of Becky's at whose house by Camas Tianavaig Mike and I had hoped to stay during our Skye circumnavigation. Andrea was a radiographer who had recently returned from a year of travelling round Asia and Australia. She was a strong paddler and had postponed embarking on her new job to slot in this trip.

We agreed to meet at Lochaline one Saturday at midday. Apart from Andrea and myself, none of us had previously met. Andrea and I shared a car from Inverness and arrived at the coffee van by the ferry slip. Wendy spotted our boats on the car and introduced herself and so began the long process of unloading the mass of gear from the cars, carrying it down to the shore and re-packing it in the boats. The tide was falling fast as we finalised our preparations, running south-east down the Sound of Mull, and, assuming that this was to be the direction of travel that afternoon, it would provide us with a push down the sound. As it would also slacken off in a couple of hours time it would allow us a perfect window of opportunity to cross the sound at low water to reach the Mull side that afternoon for the first camp. Or so we surmised!

After an hour of packing, discarding and re-packing, Joe turned up.

We helped him pack his boat, stuffing stuffed an amazing array of odd-shaped packages and parcels into his boat's holds and cockpit until no more could be crammed. But there was a problem: half his gear was still lying on the foreshore. This was apparently normal for Joe as he proceeded to stack it high on fore and aft decks, tying it down with string and bungy cords. Never before had I seen such a bizarre sight; we reckoned that the centre of gravity must have been about Joe's shoulder height as he sat in the boat. It was reminiscent of a Taiwanese boat trader carrying his goods to market – precarious and very unstable. If he were to capsize he would only rotate 90° degrees before being stopped by the deck cargo – tricky! Still he seemed happy and couldn't understand our concerns. Apart from anything else, I was intrigued to learn what on earth all these packages contained.

Mid afternoon and Joe was all set. We found space for him in his boat and launched it into the slowing south-bound tidal stream. Wendy said goodbye to her son and husband and we all pushed off ready for a few hours of paddling across the Sound to Mull to make use of the imminent slack water and the remaining daylight. I like to push on as much as possible on the first day of a trip to set the pace for the rest of the trip. This was not to be; Joe announced that we were to keep to the mainland side of the Sound of Mull and head for the bothy at Inninmore which lay 6 kilometres to the south-east of Lochaline. An hour or so of paddling! As Joe was the organiser of the trip it was not a good idea to mutiny at this early stage. We were truly disappointed not to make full use of the amazing weather and perfect tide timing to cross the sound down past Torosay and Duart castles, then on to the south coast of Mull. Instead we stopped almost as soon as we set off. The packing and unpacking of the boats was to take up far more time than we had spent on the water. The fickle Scottish weather dictates that if conditions are good it is always worth using it to make progress. On a week's trip you can almost guarantee that at least one day will be lost to impossible paddling conditions.

Still, Joe knew the bothy well and promised us a good spot nearby to camp. 'Fair do's.' We could still leave early the following morning and make up lost kilometres from this first day.

As always, the first kilometre or so of a multi-day trip somehow can be strenuous and I certainly found it a bit of a slog. Within minutes of taking to the water I looked around to see where the others were and was intrigued to see a huge empty aggregates ship coming up behind us half a kilometre further out into the sound. It was running without ballast and was enormous, its propellers half out of the water and even though it was only doing a few knots it would certainly take a long time to stop in an emergency. Despite its size and obvious power, it passed by us almost silently. As we paddled on slowly down the coast a paraglider from the cliff top to our left soared above us . The thermals rising up the cliff face in the afternoon heat caught the canopy, whisking it and the pilot higher and higher over our heads. Scared of heights, I was quite pleased to be sitting fairly and squarely on the surface of the sea. Joe watched with a critical eye. His many years of paragliding equipped him to give us a blow-by-blow account of the glider's manoeuvres aimed at using the thermal uplifts to maximum effect. Not for me, I thought, and kept focused on the choice of meal for the first night.

Soon we turned into a wide bay. Behind the thick gorse scrub, nestled in below the cliffs, sat the bothy of Inninmore, our first destination. Joe was right. It certainly was a beautiful location and despite our misgivings about the short paddle it was an excellent spot to camp with well-grazed flat grassy areas just in front of the building. With the exception of Joe's boat, we managed to carry the full kayaks, one at a time, up onto the grass above the high-water mark. When we attempted to lift Joe's, even with the combined effort of four of us, we lacked the superhuman strength required to move it more than a few feet. One of the joys of sea kayaking is that a lot more can be carried than in a rucksack on a trekking trip. Fresh fruit and vegetables, wine and other such luxuries are fairly easy to stuff into odd corners of the boat. Most boats will easily carry enough for up to ten days or so without re-stocking (apart from water) as long as a modicum of sense is employed. With this in mind, we still couldn't work out what was being transported by Joe. Para Handy's puffer could not have taken as much!

The bothy turned out to be a privately-owned house whose top floor bedroom was locked but rooms downstairs were left open for public use without charge. As we set up camp, a group of four people arrived on foot. They had been coming here on holiday for many years, hiring the top floor of the bothy from the owners and using it to escape the hustle and bustle of London. The sun would not last long as the towering cliffs behind blocked it out by mid evening and the temperatures would fall rapidly under the clear skies. The well-equipped kitchen in the bothy would have saved us from the careful juggling of pans on our camping stoves but we cooked outside to enjoy the last of the bright sun and then ate in the bothy to escape the last of the night's midges. Ensconced in the bothy the new occupants lit a fire in the kitchen hearth. The wine flowed and we passed a very pleasant evening with our bothy companions in front of the hot wood-fuelled fire in the grate. Tonight's fare on the table, pasta and tomato sauce, although not haute cuisine was enjoyable nevertheless.

It was time to head into the tents for some well-earned shut-eye; the day had been a long one even though we hadn't done much paddling. The first night of any trip is, for me, often a time of little sleep. Despite the release from work and daily chores my head can be full concerns. What would the weather be like for the week? Would we be able to complete the planned route? Would members of the group get on? Usually I wake up tired and un-rested and could easily sleep through half the following morning. Although peaceful and cold at first in the late-evening clear skies, the wind got up through the night and by 7 a.m. as we emerged from our tents, it had become a fairly strong north-westerly running down the Sound of Mull. The white-capped waves could be seen at least half way across the channel. The far side was not visible in the drizzle and low cloud, and unlike the thought of returning to the sleeping bag and a long sleep in it was not at all appealing. The crossing of the Sound was crucial to the success of the trip: no crossing, no circumnavigation. This was precisely my reason for wishing to push on the previous day whilst we had good weather and superb sea conditions. Still we had to give it a go, or at least we would once Joe emerged from his slumber. Finally setting off just before 10 a.m. we crossed Inninmore Bay, going south to the small islets of Eilean Rubha an Ridire.

These small rocky islets just metres off the west side of the southerly tip of the Morvern Peninsula are host to a series of shipwrecks, the most famous being the HMS *Dartmouth*, a 25 metre, 32 gun naval frigate, lost in 1690. Anchored off Duart Castle, she was caught by a vicious gale which dragged her across the Sound to founder on the islets at the other side. The wreck was discovered in the early 1970s and for many years a protection order was placed on it banning illegal diving activity on the remains. In the 1980s this order was, for a few years, lifted and it became a top dive site. I dived here many a time and searched the area far and wide, coming across several cannon, some of them quite a distance from the wreck itself. I wonder if they are still there. On top of part of the wreck are the remains of more modern vessels, including a fishing boat, *Ballista*, and a salvage barge. On the southern side of the islets lies the wreck of the small tug, *Girl Sandra,* and close by, *Thesis*. This last one offered a particularly good dive as it was fairly intact apart from the hull plates which lay all around, blown off the frames like a peeled banana by a local salvage diver.

Rather than take the shortest route across the channel to Mull we headed due south to Duart Castle, keeping the waves on our starboard beam in the hope that they would give a helping push across. It was rather a cruel initiation to the day and as we crossed the Sound the waves became shorter, steeper and rather noisy as they swooshed busily past down the channel. It took all our concentration to keep the boats pointing towards Duart Castle, now emerging from the mist as we bumped along in the freshening sea, while at the same time watching out for ferry traffic as we approached the mid-channel. The strong wind and waves pushed us steadily towards the castle and we became separated in rain and low visibility. I ended up by myself, entering the bay to the west of Duart Castle, which at least afforded some shelter from the wind.

It was time for the first chocolate bar of the day and a chance to grab a drink of water. I sat and waited for the others to arrive, paddle resting on the spraydeck in front of me, as the boat slopped about in the waves. Once regrouped, we dodged into the calm water below the castle and dripped out on to the nearby stone slip hewn out of the rocks. It was a moment when spirits were far from high but with a quick dart behind the rocks and a cup of hot tea from the flask some warmth briefly returned. Life was definitely worth living again.

We were now on Mull under the ramparts of the imposing castle poised for the trip 'proper' and, despite the weather, we were pleased to be here. Duart Castle, the 13th century home to the Macleans has had a turbulent history which includes it being burnt down by the Duke of Argyll in 1691, and later being confiscated after Culloden. It was bought by the 26th clan chief in 1911 and is still home to the present clan chief.

The tide, now on the flood was beginning to push up into the Sound of Mull, running headlong into the teeth of the southbound wind, which was by now howling down the channel, forcing the sea into a chaotic white-topped mess. The longer we lingered on shore the worse it would become as the tide picked up, so with some reluctance, we set off again out round the point. Though we had stopped for only ten minutes and despite the hot drink we now felt quite chilled. Within a few metres from the slip, we lost the shelter of the land and were plunged back into the turbulent grey sea. Paddling close to the rocks below the castle, the waves weren't high but they bounced back off the rocks, making for slow and very punctuated progress. This was not the most sensible of routes, but the other option was to head further out into the sound. That was less appealing as the large standing waves formed by wind against tide were very obvious just off our left shoulders. Although it was a sea state that commanded respect and the constant use of correction and low bracing strokes with the paddle to prevent capsize, it was a fairly short stretch of chaos. We soon turned south down the east coast of Mull into gradually calming seas and some respite from the wind.

Ahead of us, to the south, lay the Firth of Lorn and somewhere in the low cloud and drizzle over the channel to our left sat the island of Kerrera. Just behind it lay Oban on the mainland. Oban's nearest pub, an open fire and a steaming cup of hot chocolate were momentarily very tempting.

The coast on Mull's east side was low and relatively uninteresting as we paddled the 4 kilometres to the entrance of Loch Don. At the mouth of the narrow passage which opens up into Loch Spelve, some 5 kilometres further on, we stopped for a snack at Rubha na Faoilin. Boats dragged up onto some rocky platforms for the second time that morning, we dug eagerly into our food bags. The wind was now returning with a vengeance, funnelling through the narrow gap at the mouth of the loch. Mid-channel, we could see a spectacular line of small standing waves. Despite the weather we were pleased to have made good progress.

Back on the water we quickly powered through the short bit of bounce at the standing waves and crossed the channel. We made a fast passage down the next 10 kilometres of coast to Frank Lockwood's Island which is named after the brother-in-law of the 21st Maclean of Duart. I must admit to having no recollection of the coastline here at all and my journal for that day makes no mention of it.

From here we had decided to cross the mouth of Loch Buie and make for Carsaig Bay and call it a day there. Carsaig is a marvellous place and ideal for our second camp of the trip, although we had heard tales of camping being actively discouraged by the local laird. We hauled out on the west side of the bay, as far from the big house as we could, and found a secluded grassy spot to pitch the tents. As it was still fairly early in the afternoon, following a welcome coffee, we set off along the coastal path to visit the Nun's Cave where the nuns from Iona are reputed to have hidden during the Reformation. We came across a dank and smelly cave full of sheep droppings but we weren't sure if it was the right one. Further along the coast were the Carsaig Arches but as the path was slow-going we turned back; we would see the arches from the sea the following morning. Back at camp Andrea appeared with a miniature rugby ball and Joe produced a Frisbee. We passed the remaining hours flinging these backwards and forward, Frisbee and ball occasionally landing in soggy cow-pats. The weather was promising for the next day and the early evening shipping forecast predicted lower wind speeds than today's. With the added prospect of some sunshine as well, things were looking up.

The following day which would bring us along the southern side of the Ross of Mull. The map showed it festooned with rocky reefs and sandy coves, not to be recommended in a rough sea perhaps, but as the forecast promised fine weather, a very scenic paddle was on the cards. This stretch would complete the southern part of the island.

Missing the 5.40 a.m. shipping forecast, I slept in until 7 a.m. When at last I surfaced I found both Andrea and Wendy busy with breakfast and the very individual routine of packing the boats was underway. There is no way of speeding this process up; everything has its place and certainly, to use the old adage, there is (ultimately) a place for everything. I can never face food first thing in the morning but I usually have a coffee. A few years back a friend introduced me to an amazing cup made by Lakeland Plastics. It has a meshed insert that can be slid down a groove in the cup's side to separate the coffee grinds from the coffee, à la cafetière. I don't mind eating variations on the pasta theme day after day or eating stale bread long after its natural lifespan, but one thing that I really appreciate is half-decent coffee. Having used all manner of home-made devices, the best being a spherical tealeaf holder on a chain, to be given this marvellous, but very simple, cup was a revelation. I am frequently tempted to buy a stash of a dozen or so, just in case the company stops making them or goes bust!

The morning was a bit chilly and condensation covered the tents. The sky was clear and the day was windless and promising to be a cracker. The three of us busied ourselves with preparations for the day and were all set by 8 a.m. Still, not all was in order: Joe had not yet surfaced! There had been little conversation as we packed but as Joe was still in slumberland we began some very unsubtle loud chit-chat – to no effect. Joe stirred at 8.30, by 9 a.m. he had shown face and at 10.30 the portage down to the sea began.

Paddling along the coast to the point by the Carsaig Arches was a slog. We were chilled from hanging around the campsite and found it hard to get going. Still, the sun was up and we were enjoying the changing scenery and sandy beaches as we rounded each rocky promontory. The beaches were as good as any I had seen. Though extraordinary, they most likely seldom 'felt the footprint of man' as there was no access shown on the map. This part of Mull was truly beautiful but I suspect that the majority of visitors simply passed by as they made their way to Fionnphort to catch the ferry to Iona.

By the time we were abreast of the biggest beach, at Ardalanish Bay, it was time for the first stop. The sun was fairly warm by now, we were content with our trip and pleased that the weather was being kind to us. From here we paddled 3 kilometres south to round the headland of Rubh'

Ardalanish where we enjoyed the roar of the long lazy swell crashing up onto the rocks. We then continued due west on our planned course for the day. Seals were our constant companions, and those basking on rocks only shuffled into the water at the last moment when they lost courage, re-emerging seconds later behind the boats to check us out.

A few kilometres on we steered north-west and arrived at the tidal island of Erraid. We hadn't planned where we were to camp that day but I suppose we all thought that we would get at least as far as Iona. Never having been there before I was keen to go ashore. We turned north to see if we could navigate the channel between Erraid and the mainland of Mull but the tide was too low. We beached to see if we could carry the boats through but unfortunately it must have been a good 200 metres across or more. Although it was sunny as we stopped for lunch both Andrea and myself became very chilled. The midday breeze had a coldness to it that sapped the heat from our damp canoeing clothes. Both Joe and Wendy were wearing waterproof over trousers and were warm enough. Andrea dug out her pair; I didn't have any but Joe came to my aid and lent me his spare pair. Perhaps the excess load he was carrying wasn't a bad idea after all!

We pushed off again to paddle around Erraid but after a short distance we came across a very enticing opening at the entrance to Tràigh Gheal on the south side of the island. We turned into it to explore. The steep walls on both sides quickly opened up to reveal a first class natural anchorage, a bit shallow for yachts but a wonderful place for kayaks. The seabed was composed entirely of golden sand and above the beach at the end of the hidden bay was a series of grassy platforms, just perfect for an overnight camp. We slid over the glassy unruffled sea and went ashore to explore. Clambering up the foreshore behind the beach we noticed for the first time a second part of the inlet, also backed by a wonderful beach. In the water two people were enjoying a swim. As we stood soaking up the peaceful atmosphere of the place the swimmers emerged, stark naked and wandered up the beach to their clothes. We felt a bit guilty at chasing them away but as it was such a perfect spot we decided to stop for the night and push on to Iona the next day.

First things first; not having had a wash for the last day or two Wendy, Andrea and myself stripped off to our underclothes and raced for the water. It was, of course, breath-catchingly cold. I lasted a couple of minutes only before wimping out first. When I was dried off and changed into fresh clothes my inner body core temperature returned and I felt truly exhilarated. Here I was in a beautiful quiet spot, filled with contentment, involved in a pastime that I really enjoyed, with people of a like mind: nothing could better this.

Camp was set up in no time and we set off to explore the island. It is a small island of roughly a square kilometre. Erraid's main claim to fame is that it featured in Robert Louis Stevenson's book, *Kidnapped*, which he wrote whilst staying on the island. In some texts on Erraid this inlet that we camped in is known as Balfour's Bay.

After tea the evening passed very quickly and once all essential chores were completed I lay in my tent to read Gunter Grass's *Tin Drum*, one of my favourite books. Although I had read it a few times, to enter into it fully takes time, peace and concentration. I remember first reading it as a student whilst visiting a friend in Glasgow, sitting outside his parents' flat on a hot summer's afternoon. I was both absorbed and fascinated by the bizarre story woven by the author's warped imagination.

That night, our window of fine weather closed in the wee small hours, as it so often does. The previous day's clear blue skies and bright sun gave way the following morning to grey skies with clouds scudding quickly by, pushed by a stiff south-westerly wind of at least force 4, rising occasionally to force 5. We had been seduced by the charm of Tràigh Gheal and its hidden entrance from the south but it became obvious that this south-facing open channel posed a bit of problem. We had now to escape from it, straight into the teeth of the crashing waves and angry swell. The swell was growing minute by minute as we made busy to break camp. Once Joe appeared from his tent, breakfasted and packed his boat, we pushed off into the waves and punched our way south to the headland on our right before veering round to the west.

Soon clear of Erraid, we turned north to make our way into the Sound of Iona. The excitement was palpable. The waves crashed over the rocks all around us and although the fetch of the sea was a fair size, the tumultuous sound was not matched by danger. Running north, up the west side of Erraid, the wind and sea were now on our backs and we made very quick progress into the Sound of Iona. What a relief! Had we stayed much longer in the inlet we would have been stormbound.

The first stop of the day was to be the ferry slip on Iona. We gingerly entered the main channel to cross the sound, pleased to find the swell was now more even and the waves fairly long. Surfing down the face of each wave was a joy, albeit a bit wet, as the heavily laden bow dipped into the trough of each wave. I made a mental note to pack my tins of tomatoes and bottles of Auzzie plonk further back in the boat to let the bow resurface more easily. By the time we reached the ferry slip and nipped up the rocky foreshore we were all quite cold. Abandoning the boats in the car park, we made our way straight to the café. Sadly, our timing was unfortunate as a ferry load of American tourists beat us to the counter. When we eventually made it to the front of the queue, a large mug of hot chocolate and my favourite snack – a cheese scone – was my morning's reward. Sitting next to the radiator looking out at the wet dreich morning, hot drink in hand, was sheer bliss. The waves crashed up the seaward side of the returning ferry with a series of white explosions; it didn't look particularly safe to me. As we sat, the water from our soaking clothing dripped onto the café floor forming a rather embarrassing series of puddles below our chair legs. Not that we cared too much, although the contrast with the well-groomed Americans who did their best to ignore us was stark. Perhaps we were beyond their comprehension.

I had long wanted to visit Iona, mainly for the usual reason of visiting the long established centre for pilgrimage and religious learning; but also I was keen to visit the grave of John Smith, former leader of the Labour party taken from us so prematurely in 1994. Whilst not a Labour supporter, Smith's intelligence and moral integrity impressed me, and like many, I think that he could have become a great Prime Minister. We must have been a bit of a sight as we wandered along the road towards Iona Abbey dressed in wellies, soggy trousers, paddling cagoules and with a general air of decrepitude. The Americans watched us out of the corners or their eyes as though we had just risen from the swamp, apprehensive perhaps in case we approached them in some nefarious fashion. We kept several metres apart as we gathered outside the front door of the remarkable historic building. Unlike the Americans, we balked at the admission charge and wandered around the outside instead.

Quickly giving up as the rain became heavier I left the others and headed for a small bookshop we had passed on the way to the abbey. In the well-stocked Scottish section I continued my search of many years for a copy of Tex Geddes' *Hebridean Sharker*. After a fruitless search I asked directions to the graveyard and quickly found the gravestone of John Smith with an epitaph quoting Alexander Pope: 'An honest man's the noblest work of God.' I paid my respects, checked my watch and realised that the day was fast disappearing. We should get a move on if we wanted to keep our options open for the rest of that day's paddling. Wendy was very keen to take in Staffa on the way north up the west side of Mull. I was too, but had reservations about the weather and the sea state.

Back on the water we re-crossed the Sound of Iona, surprised at how shallow it was for most of the way; we could see the sandy bottom and kelp fronds easily despite the roughness of the water in the channel. We slipped through the anchorage at the Bull's Hole and emerged onto the topside of the Ross of Mull. To our right lay the entrance to Loch Scridain and 9 kilometres due north we could just see the cliffs of Staffa. Decision time. After a long debate on whether the sea conditions were suitable, we decided, much against Wendy's desires, to stick to the coast and to head for the island of Inch Kenneth for the night. We paddled east for 5 kilometres before swinging north to cross the mouth of Loch Scridain, rejoining the coast by the fossil tree at Rubha na h-Uamha. The tree is a fifty-million-year-old fossil, standing some 12 metres high out of the steep hillside below the high cliffs which provide a dramatic backdrop to this remote part of the Mull coast.

The crossing was pretty bouncy and I was certainly glad not to have tried for Staffa. As we approached the far side of the loch and were scanning the shoreline searching for the tree, there was a loud crack like an explosion and suddenly part of the cliff came away. Many tons of rock plunged down the hillside, becoming lodged in the scree below. Before we fully realised what was happening, it was over. As the fossil tree is a popular destination for the more adventurous visitor we hoped that no one had been anywhere near this avalanche. It was the speed of it that took me aback. It reminded me of a hill walk many years ago in the main Corrie of Slioch above Loch Maree. Two of us had been returning from the hill top heading back down the corrie in mid January when there was a sharp crack above and behind us. As we turned, a snow avalanche dumped itself on the path only 50 metres behind where we had just passed. The snow came down at a staggering speed. It was my first direct experience of an avalanche and it did not happen in the slow motion that I imagined from television clips.

We paddled on northwards, the waves gaining in strength. The wind had veered round to the west making the sea run towards us directly on to our port side. This made for slow progress as bracing strokes were necessary for the larger sets of waves which slammed into and over the boats. While it was good fun for a while, after an hour or so it was wearing. By now we were fairly well spaced out and as we gained on Inch Kenneth, Andrea and I ended up a kilometre or so offshore, mainly to avoid the clapotis which made paddling hard-going closer to the shore. We occasionally caught glimpses of Joe's and Wendy's paddle blades nearer to the shore; everyone was at least safe even if not happy at the decision to miss out Staffa. Approaching Inch Kenneth was a bit tricky as the southern entrance to the channel between it and the mainland of Mull was littered with breaking reefs which would need to be negotiated with care. Several times we stopped for a few minutes to watch the waves and get a feel for the best route to take and to gauge the right moment to make the frantic surge forward on the top of a wave so as to clear the rocks. Once in the shelter of the island we quickly landed on the sandy beach at Port an Ròin on the south-east side. The tide was low and we were forced to drag the boats through the shallows. Here and there lay edible oysters. I gathered a few to add to the evening meal but soon discarded them in case I ended up with a dicky tummy – not a pleasant prospect in a small kayak cockpit.

Camp was set up below a rocky escarpment. This would provide shelter from the wind but also enable us to keep a low profile in case of unfriendly occupants in the big house a short distance to the north of us. Inch Kenneth, currently owned by a London doctor, has no permanent residents. Prior to the Second World War it was owned by Lord Reisdale whose daughter, Unity Mitford, adored Hilter. When war finally broke out, tragically, she shot herself.

The island is only about 2 kilometres long, highest on its western side, albeit only 50 metres at the trig point. It slopes down the sheltered eastern side where the house and chapel sit. The chapel is named after Kenneth, St Columba's fellow missionary. As with nearby Iona the island was once an important ecclesiastical centre, its fertile ground providing grain for the monks of Iona.

It was late afternoon by the time we had sorted out camp and had a coffee. We set off to explore the island and first headed for the trig point on the small hill. The wind by now had gained in strength and at the top of the rise it was blowing hard buffeting us with some force. We stood at the top of the cliff high above the frothing waves below, the sea now a good force 5–6 creating white horses all around. I was glad we were on land as it would have been a bit dicey paddling in these conditions. The seas to Staffa would have been absolutely treacherous and it was just as well we did not venture that way. From our vantage position at the trig point we could see the route, weather permitting, for the following day. We would head past the islands of Gometra and Ulva, then on to the northern part of the west side of Mull before entering the top end of the Sound of Mull.

The next place to visit was the chapel and small graveyard built on the site of an earlier monastery. The chapel was in a fairly ruinous state but work was in progress to stabilise and conserve the walls. For me, the real jewel was not the chapel but the small graveyard next to it. This became the final resting place for many Highland chiefs who were interned here instead of Iona when sea conditions proved too wild for the funeral party to continue on its way. It was fairly common practice for coffin bearers to follow ancient roads to head for burial islands such as Iona or the island on Loch Shiel. Journeys could take many days or weeks when weather hindered progress. The pragmatism of coffin bearers sometimes ruled the day as delays meant the deceased could be in a pungent state of decay. The remains of a Celtic cross briefly captured our attention but the sculptured tombstones scattered around amazed us. These were in surprisingly good state despite age and exposure to the elements. One of the more recent ones depicted Sir Alan Maclean, the 22nd chief of Duart, in full armour with his dog at his feet. The atmosphere here was something special and we stood in silent respect in the howling wind, quite taken by the quality of the carved stones. We were in a way surprised that they had not been carted off to a museum or vandalised. Somehow, this graveyard was more meaningful to me than the restored buildings and artefacts of Iona. As the wind gusted around us it was easy to imagine the struggle of earlier generations living and worshipping on such a small exposed island, while producing sufficient grain to export to the bigger monastic community on Iona.

Back at the campsite I reorganised food and equipment in the holds of my boat, had a late dinner of couscous with onions and apricots, and slowly savoured the sweet delight of a Mars Bar.

Chores completed, we gathered below a large rocky escarpment just above the camp to discuss plans for the next day. It would be relatively easy to move on to Ulva even in the present weather, as our island would provide shelter. Nevertheless, without some improvement in the conditions we probably couldn't go much further than that. As the evening wore on the wind eased slightly and we had high hopes that we wouldn't be delayed too much. As darkness set in, and the warmth of our sleeping bags was in our thoughts, Joe nipped down to his boat and reappeared with a large plastic box and a cardboard tube. With a flourish and short speech, he announced that it was his 50th birthday that day and his wife had made him a cake: not some mini, easy to carry affair, but a full-size job complete with icing and decorations.

What an amazing place to have a birthday. The cake was delicious – and now we had some explanation for his large deck bags. Even more wonderful were the contents of the cardboard tube: a fine bottle of malt. When, sometime later, replete and a bit woozy, we retired, sleep was instant and peaceful.

Morning dawned bright with clear skies. The weather seemed to be taking a turn at wind and cloud one day, then sun and settled conditions the next. Somehow there was no need to rush off this morning. We had enjoyed our brief visit to the island and were loath to leave. Back on the water we paddled north a kilometre or two to reach the channel at Ulva ferry which separates Mull from Ulva. The nearby land to the left of the narrow channel was covered in a dense layer of ferns, brambles, scrub and stunted trees in stark contrast to the heather-covered, browsed land on the Mull side of the channel.

Sadly, many parts of Scotland have been vandalised by over grazing by deer and sheep. The beauty of rugged Highland landscapes, so loved by many, is a sad legacy of many decades of gross mismanagement by landowners and misguided government policies. Whilst the scenery of the hills and glens is quite magnificent, it is enhanced a thousand fold by remnants of the ancient forests of Caledonia. Land that could nurture diverse flora has been abused for eight decades by vast strands of planted coniferous monocultures. A lot has been written about this but nothing puts it more succinctly than the acronym – MAMBA, Miles And Miles of Bugger All. Only in a few places have people had the insight to plant and enhance native forests or allow trees to survive out of reach of the tree-gobbling deer and grazing sheep. Small islands in the middle of highland lochs, or offshore islands like Ulva, despite some deer, have not been denuded of all greenery and are strikingly beautiful.

As we sat on the wall above the small harbour on Ulva, steaming coffee from the tearoom in our hands, we soaked in the ever-strengthening morning sun. Ulva, or 'Wolf Island' was once home to some 800 people who managed to make a good living from its fertile soil and on good years managed to export a surplus of potatoes. However, in 1845, over two thirds of the population was itself 'exported' by a new owner to make way for sheep. Ulva is the base of the MacQuarrie clan, one of whom, General Lachlan MacQuarrie, became the 'father of Australia' where he is celebrated to this day in statues and road names.

From Ulva we had a short day's paddling to bring us round the north-west side of Mull to rejoin the Sound of Mull. We were in no hurry when we finally set off again to skirt the north sides of Ulva and Gometra. Initially we kept to the middle of Loch Tuath but as we approached the stunning waterfall at Eas Fors we struck out for the north side and then kept close to the shore as far as the small sandy beach of Tràigh na Cille where we went ashore for a break. This was a little tricky as there was a short sharp choppy sea developing and the shore was littered with rocky shoals. From here we looked due west to the Treshnish Islands, which were sharply silhouetted in the clear daylight. From this bay there was a 9 kilometres paddle to round Treshnish Point.

For the first few kilometres it was an enjoyable paddle but as we pulled clear of the shelter of Gometra and headed out into the more exposed part of the coast, the waves grew steadily in height. By the time we began turning north to make for the headland the south-westerly swell from the previous day's strong wind was rolling in on our left side at quite some pace and growing in height by the minute. As usual, we had omitted to make our tidal calculations and the ebbing tide was now running south against the direction of the prevailing sea. Paddling forward became slower and slower as most of the effort was required to keep balance in the steep-sided swell which had now grown to a good 3 metres in height. Close to our right the swell boomed and exploded into white froth as it collided with the cliffs. We were initially too close to the backwash and the clapotis was a serious hazard to watch out for. All the same, there is a certain psychological comfort in being close to land in a big sea, even though you know that if anything went wrong, there would be no chance of surviving in the murderous surge on the rocks.

We stayed pretty close together in case one of us tipped over, but that too presented problems as several times one of the boats would suddenly surge down the face of a large wave and almost collide with another. At least the sea was, in the main, following us so that there was no need to maintain a hard forward effort to paddle up each oncoming wave. Once you were in the trough and all else was blotted out from view apart from the grey wall of water all around, all you could do was sit and wait for the next roller to come behind and lift the boat up the great elevator until you were perched high again and able to smile weakly or call to the others who happened to be on the same part of this free roller-coaster ride.

Just when we thought we had mastered this sea and the coast was beginning to turn into Calgary Bay, the southbound tide became stronger and the clash of this against southwesterly rollers aggravated the sea conditions. The seas grew by another metre or more. This increase alone would have been acceptable but the waves became very steep-sided. Each time one gathered up behind the stern of the boat you felt that you were in danger of being turned somersault – stern over bow. Enjoyment was fast giving way to fear as I surfed down the face of each wave with a hard brace to keep the boat from broaching. I was a bit gripped and waited for each wave to begin to pick the boat up, then back-paddle for all I was worth to slow down the headlong acceleration into the trough and the strong possibility of being totally trashed in the process. My mouth was dry and although I had a drinking tube to hand I was too tense to use it.

This was one of the few times I have felt seasick in a kayak; I think it was the tremendous noise of the breaking waves as well as the size of the sea that was getting to me. From the corner of my eyes I could see, close by me, Andrea and Wendy paddling fairly tightly together and after a few seconds of panic searching, Joe could be seen some 10 metres further offshore, paddling with his seemingly lackadaisical style, as though his only thought in the world was what flavour of jam to put in his sandwich that lunchtime! Was it me being a total wimp in these conditions? By now I was keen to get out of this sea and was very relieved to arrive at the headland and turn the boat towards the beach at Calgary. From here the influence of the tide waned and the swell began to lose its power.

We regrouped and pottered in for lunch at the sands in front of us. Wendy and I landed first, followed by Joe, then Andrea. The sea now had lost all its strength and only small surf was left to break innocuously on the beach. As Andrea made her final steering correction stroke to prepare to land, a larger wave suddenly appeared unexpectedly, caught the stern of her boat and whisked it round just as the bow touched the shore. The result was an unavoidable capsize and she was unceremoniously tipped onto the hard sand in a couple of inches of water. Ridiculous, but it was the trigger to release all my tensions and as I helped to drain the water (and an enormous amount of marine life) out of her cockpit, I couldn't help but laugh out loud at the absurdity of the situation – survived the big sea but trashed on the sandy beach. A family of tourists wandered along the waterline and one of the children splashed at the water's edge. We felt a bit amateurish as we sorted Andrea's boat out – little did they know of our 'iffy' rounding of the headland, which, from here looked like nothing at all.

Calgary Bay is immortalised in contemporary Scottish history as one of the places from which people were evicted and forced to leave their homeland for distant shores during the Highland Clearances in the middle of the 19th century. Ironically, it was around the time that many viewed slavery as an abomination of human rights. The rights of Scottish crofters obviously did not rate highly in these first stirrings of colonial guilt. Whilst I would never condone the actions of the estate owners and their factors, much of the development of the new world at this time in history was facilitated by displaced Scots. Our own Westminster Government only woke up to the consequence of the Clearances a few decades later when there were so few young Scottish men left to provide cannon fodder for the trenches of the First World War.

We abandoned the boats along the water's edge, all off us too tired to carry them higher up the beach. Big rocks to hide behind for calls of nature were a bit hard to find but one by one we sneaked off and made the best of what was there. Then, after a series of trips to and from the boats we assembled our food and flasks. Lunch was a real pleasure in the sun. All around we had draped our soggy wet outer kayaking clothes on the rocks to dry. Even though we were glad to be here and safe at last, Calgary Bay was not our final destination for the day and we still had the psychological challenge of reaching the final northwesterly headland of Caliach Point, some 5 kilometres to our north, and of rounding it before we would enter the shelter of the sound. Treshnish Point had been a real shock to us, as we had not expected problems. However, Caliach Point was the headland about which we had heard stories of big seas. Certainly, on the map it did jut out, and could prove hazardous.

As we chatted about what to do next we realised that this was a biggy! If we rounded the headland today, we would crack the trip. If we failed and the weather turned against us, we were stuffed and might have to give up right here. Despite the state of the sea we had no real option but to go back out and paddle round the final major headland. The boats were still at the water's edge where we had left them. The tide had now dropped as far as it was going to and it would be on the turn shortly. The significance of this did not dawn on us as we pushed off again. I don't know about the others, but I was very nervous about this next stage of the journey. We paddled a bit hesitantly out towards the mouth of the bay; to the north side was a series of rock reefs against which the sea was repeatedly breaking heavily with an almighty roar and wash of foam. We looked for a through-route between two of the biggest outcrops but could not identify one. We had no choice but to turn briefly towards the southwest, straight into the big sea before turning north once we were clear of the reefs. Caliach Point headland was 3.5 kilometres north. This was it: make or break. The sea was still swollen as we weighed into the open Atlantic. I decided to paddle out, away from the cliffs to try to avoid the reflection of the waves bouncing back from the rocks. The others stayed within a couple of hundred metres of the cliffs. The waves were still big but without the counterforce of the ebbing tide.

It dawned on me that the tide had turned and that the previously opposing forces of wind and tide meeting at Treshnish Point were now working in the same direction. I breathed a deep sigh of relief. I was too far away to shout across to the others but they too seemed to be paddling well and without apparent difficulties. I carried on, at ease at last, in my offshore route. I was now enjoying the sea and looked forward to each big wave picking my kayak up stern first and surfing down the face until

I stalled the boat as the wave passed on by at a tangent to the direction I was heading. The headland was now approaching fast and, my earlier tension now gone, I was nevertheless very aware that rounding the point could be the real test of our skills.

At this point of the island the long-running ocean swells met the strong currents now being funnelled up the Sound of Mull by the flooding tide. This interaction might lead to enormous waves and I was concerned at how bad it could be. No matter how often I encounter difficulties paddling through a wild sea, I don't become more confident, just more aware of how vulnerable sea kayakers are. I decided to keep further out than the others in the more regular movement of the swell, in case the conditions worsened. At the same time I was impatient to reach the headland to get this over with, come what may. Finally, the headland was off my starboard beam and I turned right to close in on it and to rejoin Andrea, Joe and Wendy, who were also at the same latitude albeit a little closer to the shore. At this juncture I realised that I was too far out and the paddle to gain the headland would be a slog with the sea on the right of my boat's stern. What the hell! I could see round the headland and I was going for it. Ten minutes of hard paddling was all it took to catch up with the others and to round the point.

The worsening conditions which we had expected had not materialised. The relief was immense as we pottered along in the now flattening seas. Talk was only of where we could land and set up camp. The shore was rather uninviting but 3 kilometres further along the sandy beach at Port Langamull appeared, and without discussion we pulled in to abandon the sea for the day. From here Tobermory was only a half day's paddle away. My only recollection of that evening was of having a quick meal and crawling into my sleeping bag as soon as I could. I was exhausted and much-needed sleep was my priority to replenish my energy. Tomorrow could not possibly be as hard as today.

I awoke early again and lay for a while listening to heavy rainfall thudding on my tent. Even though I had pitched the tent in a fairly sheltered part of the grass above the beach, I was aware of the blustery wind. There was no great incentive to rise and face the day. However, the prospect of soon being in Tobermory forced me to emerge from the warmth and comfort of my sleeping bag. Once again, Wendy and Andrea were already up and preparing to set off. I quickly boiled water for my flask and to make coffee and then set about packing the boat.

As Joe was not up by the time we were ready I left the flysheet of my tent still in position and the three of us crouched inside to keep the worst of the wind and rain off us while we waited for him to surface.

Eventually Joe made an appearance, breakfasted, packed his boat and we set off to paddle the 16 kilometres to Tobermory, a distance that should take around two-and-a-half hours. We should arrive by lunchtime. No sooner had we left the shelter of the bay than we realised that today was going to be tough. The wind was howling from the south and south-east with a vengeance. The gusts, one after the other, hit us hard. By watching the sea surface ripple along the wind front we could tell when the next gust was coming. Gripping the paddles tightly we braced ourselves for the impact. After each gust we would paddle hard to make some ground before stopping for the next one. As the wind was pushing us offshore we headed as close in to the rocky sea edge as we could to gain some shelter from the elements. A short distance offshore the winds were whipping the sea into reasonable-sized waves. When after about one kilometre we turned into to the mouth of Loch a' Chumhainn we decided to cross to the other side rather than lengthen our route by paddling in the relative shelter up the mouth before crossing. This proved to be a task and a half. The wind was being funnelled up the loch and paddling was almost impossible. Each time the paddle blade was lifted above shoulder height it would catch the wind and try to wrench itself out of my grasp. Forward progress was slow and a huge effort was necessary to counter the wind which was pushing us north at a surprising rate.

One event supplied some mirth to this otherwise hard graft. As I slowly gained the other side of the loch I headed into the shelter of a stretch of cliff. Just below it, a seal was bobbing about in the water fast asleep. Only its snout emerged as it drifted in the calm water. I stopped paddling and allowed the forward momentum of the boat to carry me right up to it, then gave it a quick tap on its snout with my paddle blade. It momentarily opened its eyes, closed them again, then opened them wide in disbelief. In panic it almost leapt clean out of the water as it fled off, covering me in spray. It popped up a few metres away and gave the dirty look I deserved.

An easy morning paddle into Tobermory was not to be. I much preferred yesterday's big sea to this torture. For the next two hours we battled along the coast. As we approached the most northerly point of Mull at Ardmore the scenery to our right was very impressive. The steep slopes and cliffs were quite spectacular and the trees and shrub cover was good to see again as most of the island was covered in heather. Realising that once round Ardmore Point we would be facing directly into the oncoming gale, we stopped for a snack and to gather our reserves. We felt as if we had been paddling all day. With some reluctance we turned the corner and headed south-east. This was no joke at all. The wind was ferocious and made forward progress almost impossible. Had the shelter of Tobermory not now been so close we would have given up for the day. Each metre paddled was fought for against the wind. If you stopped paddling for even a moment, to take a drink or catch your breath, the boat would stop dead in the water and immediately begin to get blown back the way it had come.

We eventually entered Bloody Bay (the name on the map – not how we felt towards it). The Bay was less than a kilometre wide but it must have taken a good hour to cross. Although we could now see the lighthouse at Rubha na Gall which lay only 2 kilometres north of Tobermory, it was to be a long slow paddle to get to it. Bizarrely, or so it seemed to us anyway, as we made our approach towards the lighthouse, a large white cruise ship appeared from the north and stopped mid channel, then began to launch small cutters to transport its guests into Tobermory. They were ungainly little craft and made slow progress in the substantial sea that had developed in the main channel.

At last we passed the lighthouse and turned due south to claw our way into the harbour and shelter. What an epic journey! Now 3 p.m., it had taken us approximately six hours to reach this point and we were shattered, cold and a bit fed up – time to hit the nearest tearoom.

A couple of hours later we were rested and ready to set up camp if we could find somewhere near at hand. We pottered along the edge of the bay, stopping for a few moments to take some pictures of each other below the waterfall at Sput Dubh, which falls over a small cliff straight into the sea. With no sign of a campsite on the mainland we crossed over to the south of Calve Island and pulled up on a sheltered bit of low land between Calve and its little satellite island of Cnap a' Chailbhe where we managed to find just enough space for the four tents on the top of the salt marsh. As we were setting up camp I noticed out of the corner of my eye a movement down by the shore. A pair of mink emerged and flitted past, moving very fast along the seaweed-covered rocks.

Calve Island is uninhabited these days but some decades ago two intrepid canoeists, Alastair Dunnet and James (Sèumas) Adam, stayed here with the farmer and helped with chores for a while. Their story is a Scottish adventure classic, *The Canoe Boys* by Alastair Dunnet. Since then the fields of Calve Island have pretty much reverted to bog and reed and are now home to a few sheep, its people now sadly gone.

This would be our last night of the trip as the following day we would complete the circumnavigation by paddling down the Sound of Mull and crossing over to rejoin our cars at Lochaline. Despite the hardship of the last two days it had been a great trip and we were a little sad at the thought of our holiday coming to an end. For the first time we built a campfire. Twenty minutes or so of gathering driftwood and bits of old pallet from the shore we got the fire going, albeit a little smokily. As we sat round staring at the flames discussing the past few days and future plans, Joe dug out his cardboard tube and dispensed some much-welcomed whisky again. Later, as the fire died down, the wind picked up and our merriment was blighted by the occasional rain shower. Time to call it a night.

Although the wind blew through the night and the odd gust hit the tent with a bang and shudder, by morning it had all but blown itself out and the day was bright and the sea still a little lively in the sound. We were greatly heartened by this turn in the weather, as a repeat of the previous day would have been too much for us. Almost as a dare to the weather I did not put on my windproof cagoule as we set off. As the day wore on it got better and better – the wind died away and the sun had some warmth in it.

The 20 kilometres down the sound were uneventful. We stopped for lunch at the promontory of Rubh an t-Sean Chaisteil and spend a while with no success searching for the ancient broch that was marked on the map. From here we cut across the sound to the Morvern side. In the early afternoon sun the last few kilometres were a real joy. We paddled some distance apart, ambling along close to the coast, watching out for otters and other wildlife that seemed to abound along here. Our thoughts were occupied by the last five days of paddling. It had been a good trip and we were very fortunate not to have been shore bound by the poor weather. Although we had completed the circumnavigation of Mull, there were many places we had passed that we wanted to come back to and explore. I would like to paddle round Iona, but a kayaker's tale would deter me from camping on it. He had camped on the island and when he returned from a walk his tent was gone. As he looked around he could see a car leaving the area so he gave chase. Sure enough, his gear was in the car and the driver, a rather crusty matronly lady, gave him a telling off for daring to camp on Iona. He in turn gave her a ticking off for stealing his equipment and camping gear.

By the time we pulled past the old pier just before Lochaline and paddled into the place from where we had launched five days ago almost to the hour, the following year's trip to Ulva, Gometra and out to Staffa had been conceived.

Best meal on trip: Mexican rice 'n' beans

1 can of red kidney beans, drained
1 onion, chopped
2 cloves garlic, sliced
Cooking oil
1 tablespoon flour
2 teaspoons of ground cumin
1 teaspoon chilli powder
Vegetable stock cube
1 cup basmati rice
Butter

Cook the rice with twice as much water as rice. Put to one side. Fry the garlic and onion until soft, then add the beans and heat. Add the vegetable stock cube and a little water. Mix the butter, flour and cumin to form a paste. Stir, taking care to avoid lumps. Simmer for 20 minutes until the mixture thickens like gravy. Serve with Tabasco sauce and wash down with a cool lager.

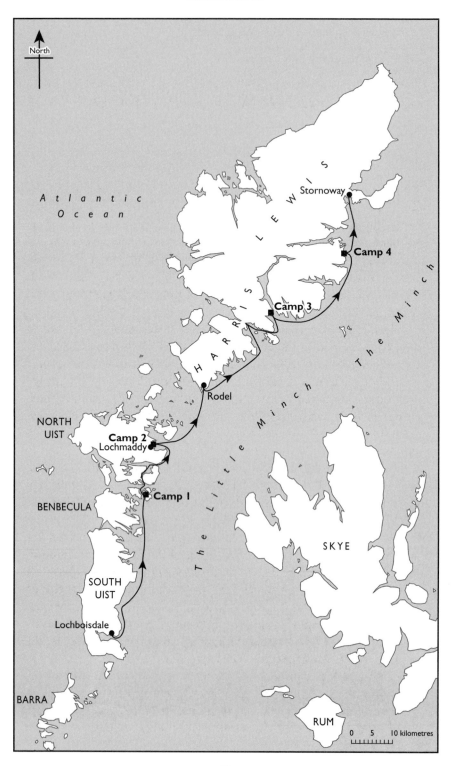

Chapter 3

Lochboisdale to Stornoway

Having been thwarted in our attempt to cross to Norway for a week's paddling, Andrea and I decided to stay in Scotland and head west instead to paddle the east side of a section of the Western Isles from Lochboisdale to Stornoway, a distance of 130 kilometres. Whilst this was a reasonable distance to paddle in the time available, it was some 80 kilometres short of the full length of the chain of islands and sounds stretching in latitude from the north tip of the Scottish mainland to the Ardnamurchan peninsula in the south.

We discounted routes which would have taken us to the west side of the islands for part of the way in case westerly winds stopped progress for too long. Simply circumnavigating one or two of the islands and spending time ashore enjoying the hills and beaches was an attractive proposition, but in the end we gambled on the east side being sheltered enough to allow us to make the most of our time, although we did expect to be stormbound for at least one day, as is so often the case even on a short trip.

Despite being tempted at the last minute to deviate from our original plans because of a forecast of south-west gales in sea areas Malin and Hebrides we set off from Dingwall on Saturday morning bound for Oban and the ferry to Lochboisdale. Whilst taking cognisance of weather forecasts is eminently sensible, the old proverb, 'nothing ventured – nothing gained' is also worth considering. I have often backed down from a trip because of a poor weather forecast only to find out afterwards that the bad weather didn't come in as soon as forecasters first indicated or else passed quickly! Should the worst come to the worst there were many attractive walks on the Uists to keep us occupied for a few days.

We arrived at Oban's south pier and began packing the boats. By the time we were ready and had left the car with a friend of Andrea's, it was time to board the CalMac ferry. We were ushered to the front of the queue and shuffled down the linkspan into the cavernous car deck to deposit the boats at the far end of the vessel. When both boats were securely tied down the other vehicles were let on.

The crossing past Mull and across the Minch was fairly smooth, which was surprising considering the forecast. I left Andrea, tired from the long drive, to sleep in the observation lounge and made my way out on to the aft deck. I passed the time watching out for whales and dolphins and chatted to an Irish chap who worked during the week in Glasgow as a drug rehabilitation worker but, come the weekend, returned to his wife and family at his adopted home in Benbecula. Although commuting weekly like this was not easy, it was essential in order to unwind from his job and to keep him sane. We stood for most of the trip leaning on the rails, not saying much but appreciating the views of Mul, then Coll and Tiree off to the south. I suspect that whilst my job was not as stressful as his, we both saw the journey across the Minch as a chance to discard the hassles of work, time-keeping and mundane existence.

An hour out from Oban, a pod of three or four bottle-nosed dolphins appeared off to the left, a hundred metres or so behind the ferry, and crossed our wake on their way south. Aware of our presence they did not deviate from their course at all: ferry and dolphins sharing the same water in two very different worlds. Seeing these beautiful creatures made my final task at work before setting off seem such a banal waste of time; I had been filling out performance statistics for biological samples and time spent analysing each sample! Yet, what clearly mattered in this environment were the dolphins themselves. We are only here in this planet for a few decades so why do we make things so difficult for ourselves? I asked my fellow traveller if this was because we, as the human race, were simply too numerous and had become too detached from life's essentials. We humans have to 'compete' with each other in order to show that we have some importance and ultimately end up carrying out tasks of little relevance to life. Not only do many of our race resort to taking drugs to escape from the reality of daily existence, we also have people in place to wean them off again. Where is the fundamental issue here?

The cold and wind brought us back to reality: he to the bar for a pint and a nip, and me to the lounge to read the *Scotsman* from cover to cover. I would not see another edition until I reached Tarbert later in the week. I remember a few years back going into a small shop on South Uist and asking for a newspaper. The assistant straightaway asked if I wanted that day's or the previous day's? I naturally said, 'Today's'. 'Come back tomorrow,' I was told. Such was the speed of delivery in this part of the world. Does another day make one whit of difference, I wondered.

It was good to be here removed from essential daily tasks. Even better would be the kayaking trip itself, whatever the weather brought. I love being away from mundane surroundings: lying in a tent with a cup of tea listening to the sounds of the wind and rain outside is peace in itself. I use the word 'love' with due consideration as it does indeed reflect the state of well being felt at these moments. How often have I been storm bound on a lonely part of the west coast, the seas crashing on the nearby shore, unable to carry on with the journey? In situations like these, there is absolutely nothing you can do other than accept the conditions and hole-up in the tent, waiting for a break in the weather.

One such trip was with a party from the Mallaig Canoe Club. We had gone from Arisaig to Eigg, Muck and then Sanna Bay on the topside of the Ardnamurchan Peninsula. That evening the weather turned pretty poor and bore in from the north-west. The following morning, Sunday, Roger, our trip leader, decided that we were to remain put as the conditions were too bad to travel on back to Ardtoe to the cars. However, I had to get to a work meeting in Perth on Monday morning. I declared that I would paddle on by myself to finish the trip that day. I was more that happy to do this and did not wish to inflict my decision on others. Roger eventually decided to push on too and the party was galvanised. We broke out of the beach into a large sea and, with the wind and sea on our backs, headed back to our rendezvous point at Ardtoe. It was a hairy trip and I have always felt rather guilty at pushing Roger into keeping the party together, and I suppose also watching out for me. It is fair to say though that the whole party, including me, learned some new paddling skills that day as we surfed down the waves and as a group looked after each other in arduous conditions – although I was not sure about Jon Watt's broach across a big wave face to become stuck on top of my kayak's bow. Frantic bracing by us both avoided a serious ducking!

The ferry called first at Castlebay, the main settlement on the Isle of Barra, to let off some passengers and a couple of cars, then headed north to make the short trip up the coast to Lochboisdale where it would berth for the night. By the time we arrived at our final destination it was 9.30, dark, and to top it all, it was raining. As we stood in the car deck by our boats waiting for the ferry to dock a chap came across to chat and to ask what our plans were. He had a holiday home on the island and loved the sea. As the ferry bumped to a halt against the pier he wished us good luck with our venture before joining his family in the landrover. We let the other cars off first so as not to hinder them, then carried the boats off the vessel and sat them on the quayside while we decided where to set up camp. One of the ferry crew pointed us to a bit of grass behind the tourist office which was used as an unofficial campsite. The only problem was that this was a good 200 metres away along the main road; it would take forever to carry two fully laden kayaks that far – oh for a pair of wheels! Once again, CalMac came to the rescue: we scrounged a four-wheel trolley from the ferry. We scooted along the main street in the rain, with me pulling the trolley laden with both boats and Andrea hanging on to them to stop them bouncing off. Thankfully, no cars came along and no one noticed this strange vehicle. When we arrived at the bit of rough grass behind the small tourist office there were several other tents already there. With a sigh of relief we slotted our two in as well, plus the kayaks. It was well after 11 p.m. by the time we were organised and sleep came quickly.

Next morning we were up and off early, trying to make as little noise as possible so as not to disturb others in their tents. We were on the water by 8 a.m. The weather was perfect: no wind and the promise of clear skies and some sunshine. As we picked our way past the moored boats in the inner harbour some fish-farm workers were busy loading their landing craft with bags of fish feed. One hailed us to ask where we were heading. His only retort when we shouted back 'Stornoway' was 'Mad bastards!' Hopefully we weren't and we paddled on leaving the harbour far behind. After 2–3 kilometres we emerged out of the loch and turned north. The ferry appeared off our right-hand side and slid back to Oban; there was no one on deck to wave to and strangely, I felt very alone and removed from events. Although Andrea was only 50 metres or so ahead at this point, her presence didn't diminish this odd feeling. I wondered if we had bitten off too much for this journey; after all Stornoway was a long way to the north and we had to cross the reputedly treacherous Sound of Harris half way through the journey – perhaps the fish farm worker was right.

There is little access by road to the east side of South Uist. No one lives on this side and apart from the impact of sheep grazing, the environment is as pristine as it is likely to be anywhere in Britain. The first habitation we would arrive at would be a small collection of houses at the mouth of Loch Skipport, 25 kilometres to the north of us.

To our right the sun was rising steadily and the air was warming up. It wasn't going to be a hot day but it promised to be very pleasant for paddling. Little by little my anxiety faded and I began to look forward to the journey.

We passed through a narrow channel between the island of Stulaigh and South Uist and then a couple of kilometres further on we crossed the mouth of Loch Ainort. To the north-west the land rose rapidly to the high mountains that form a prominent backbone to the island. Many of the hill names date back to Norse times when Viking travellers used these hills as navigational landmarks; names such as Hecla and Eaval are very different to the Gaelic place names all around. It was easy to visualise fleets of longships passing through these waters causing great fear amongst the indigenous people of the area. Apart from the sheep dotting the hillsides, little would have changed here since the times of the Viking conquests many centuries before.

North of Ainort the coast was indented by several large bays and we kept close to the rocky shore to watch out for otters. By twelve o'clock it was time for lunch and we drew up on the only sandy beach we came across on the entire island, at Bàgh Uisinis. Andrea had been here before and had stayed at a small bothy up the hillside. Although it was marked on the map, it was at first almost impossible to locate. After a ten-minute tramp through soggy peat bog followed by thick heather we came to the low stone structure. Inside it was well maintained but judging by the bothy's book it was little used. Many of the entries were by other sea kayakers following routes similar to our own. We found Andrea's entry from two years before but as we weren't staying over, we didn't add our own message to the book.

After lunch we travelled east for 2 kilometres out of the bay, then resumed our northerly track again. The rocky shoreline developed into steep cliffs some 20–30 metres high as we headed for the Uisinish Lighthouse which stood perched above the sea on the cliff top above us. There is no land access to this lighthouse and it must have been a remote posting for the keepers before it was automated. As we rounded the point below the lighthouse we could see a boat in the distance, sitting a few kilometres out to sea. On board we could just make out a group fishing off its aft deck. These were to be the first and only people we were to see that day. As we paddled north we would pass inshore of the boat but a few minutes later it started up and turned in towards us. The skipper was none other than the man we had talked to on the ferry car deck the previous day. He and his family were fishing for mackerel and after a chat about weather and sea conditions they offered us part of their catch. Some fish were stuffed into a plastic bag and dropped down to us. Andrea prised back her spraydeck and slipped the bag into her cockpit. We thanked them and paddled on, pleased to have been given some fresh food for that night's meal. There was a slight problem, however. The fish were still half alive, twitching against Andrea's legs. She tore open her spraydeck and hauled out the bag of fish. Once they were safely stowed on deck we set off again and half an hour later came to the mouth of Loch Skipport. Although there was a road and houses somewhere to our left we steered well clear and preferred to push on as conditions were good. We were now approaching the north end of South Uist. Only 10 kilometres away to the west was the army missile testing range, where we would encounter some problems a couple of years later.

But now we were 'on a roll', wallowing in ideal kayaking conditions. The light was wonderful; the sun was slightly covered by high thin cloud, strangely diffusing its light, but all land features were perfectly highlighted. We quickly crossed the island-strewn passage between South Uist and Benbecula, arriving on the other side between the island of Wiay and Loch Chill Eireabhraigh and finally emerging out again into the Minch via Loch a Laip. I have no recollection at all of the island of Benbecula but after a couple of hours we had passed it by and arrived at a channel between the islands of Grimsay and Ronay which lie immediately south of North Uist. It was now late in the afternoon and we had made a respectable 46 kilometres. Time to call it a day. We hauled out onto the small island of Garbh Eilean Mòr and set up camp for the night. I had had very little fluid that day and suddenly felt a desperate need to drink. I boiled a pan of water on the Trangia and dug out my Strawberry and Blackcurrant tea bags to make a massive brew. Dinner was early that evening and when we had eaten we climbed the small hill behind the camp to watch the sun sink behind Grimsay: the perfect end to a marvellous day of paddling. We were off to a good start and we both felt fit and keen to push on as far as possible the following day.

Next morning the skies were grey and leaden, the wind howling above the sheltered dip in front of the hill where we were camped. It was coming from the north-east, the worst possible direction for our passage up the east side of North Uist. As we breakfasted, we didn't discuss the day ahead but set off as soon as we could in case the wind worsened. For the first 2 kilometres we were fairly sheltered by Ronay to our right. At its north-west tip we ran foul of a large area of shallow water and, as the tide was pretty low, dense beds of kelp made paddling through the fronds hard work.

As soon as we emerged into the small sea loch leading out to the Minch at Flodaigh Beag we were hit by the full blast of the wind. It drove squalls through the narrow gap between the island and the mainland of North Uist. We watched each one approach and as they hit us we leaned forward and tried to keep the paddles low while still using them as much as possible to stop ourselves being pushed back the way we had just come by the wind. The next 3 kilometres were an absolute slog but we eventually reached the entrance to the loch. From here the next major inlet was Loch Maddy. This was only 10 kilometres away but there were no places to land other than at Loch Ephoirt, 5 kilometres up the coast.

From our vantage point behind a low reef at the narrow gap at the mouth of the loch we sat and watched the big white-capped seas rushing straight towards us, breaking over the rocks in front of us with impressive force. It didn't look good. What worried us was the danger of heading up the coast and being caught out in worsening conditions with no place to run to for shelter. I took an exploratory paddle out into the seas and within a minute or so gave up. It was desperately hard work with the nose of the boat ploughing hard into the face of each wave, climbing up and over the peak before plunging heavily into the trough of the next. The short, steep shape and size of the waves were such that each one rolled right along the top decks of my heavily laden kayak and slammed hard against my upper body. This was tiring and forward progress was going to be impossible. The wind was also much stronger out here and it was clear that reaching Lochmaddy that day by this route was not going to be feasible. I stopped paddling forward and allowed myself to be blown backwards, back into the shelter of the rocks to rejoin Andrea.

Following from yesterday's great paddle we were somewhat dejected at being thwarted so early on the second day; we didn't want to give up and set up camp again. We felt so positive about the trip that we had to somehow push on. Just to our north stood Eaval, the highest hill on North Uist and whilst it was only 347 metres high, it stood head and shoulders above the low flat land that is a feature of this island. The island is laced with a myriad of freshwater lochans, so much so that within North Uist there is probably as much water as there is land. As we drifted back towards the west, blown steadily by the wind on our backs, it dawned on us that this network of freshwater lochs could be our salvation. A brief look at the map showed that it might be possible to reach Lochmaddy by the 'overland' route via the lochans. If nothing else it would keep us occupied for a few hours.

On the map there was a long narrow sea loch extending some 2 kilometres into the middle of the island. This would be the way into our new route. As we entered the narrow channel the tide was still ebbing; the water was flowing fast out of the channel making paddling 'upstream' difficult. The low tide was a problem as the channel was very shallow and we didn't have enough time to reach a landing point in water to make our first portage. Undaunted, for the last 100 or so metres we dragged the boats over the muddy shallows to reach the north shore. Thankfully, the place we arrived at had a peaty, mud banking and after a lot of shoving, slipping and cursing, the boats were heaved up onto the moor. We had decided to head for the biggest freshwater loch called Loch Obsaraigh as this would take us the bulk of the way overland to rejoin the sea at Loch Euphoirt.

The map showed a small narrow lochan just over the moor from where we had heaved the boats up from the sea below. This small loch would take us to within 50 metres of Obsaraigh but first we had to get the boats and ourselves to the lochan. In our Scott-of-the-Antarctic mode we fashioned our tow ropes into two harnesses, clipped ourselves onto the bow of the first boat and dragged it over the heather-covered moor. This turned out to be surprisingly efficient as the thick, wet heather made for a fairly slippery surface to slide the boats over. Not so were the various peat hags that we slopped and slithered through, the boat careering sideways on several occasions dragging us off our feet and into the peaty slop. It only took forty minutes to transfer each boat and we were ready to take to the water again.

The first small lochan was shallow and paddling through water lilies provided a novel experience. At the far end there was an old fence to pass the boats over before joining the bigger loch. The wind was still very strong and above us stood the brooding presence of Eaval, now dubbed Evil, and in our banter it became the malevolent force behind our current difficulties. We reckoned it had seen our good progress the previous day and had decided mischievously to give us a hard day.

Once in Loch Obsaraigh, despite the wind, paddling was relatively easy, the smaller waves slopping against our sides. From the north end of the loch the map indicated a short distance on land to regain the sea. When we couldn't find the exit burn from the loch, which we had planned to slide the boats down, we reconnoitred the route overland again. It was only a couple of hundred metres to the nearest point of the sea in Loch Euphoirt but the tide was still out and where we were was high and dry. Not wanting to damage the hulls of the boats by dragging them over the sandy flats of the dried-out bay, we hauled them over the heather around the bay to a bit of bedrock just above the water from where we could launch again. This took a long time as there were numerous dips and small burns to negotiate. The effort left us thoroughly exhausted as the boats were fully laden and heavy.

We knew by repute that the very narrow entrance of Loch Euphoirt had strong currents and as the tide would soon be on the turn and would also have the sea driving it, we were eager to make our passage out of the loch before the currents picked up. At this point we had decided to head out to sea, come hell or high water. Although the overland portages and freshwater paddles had been successful we determined to do some proper sea paddling again.

Out in the Minch, the wind had moderated a notch or two and the seas were not as ferocious as they had been earlier in the day. We had only 5 kilometres to paddle to reach Loch nam Madadh. Initially it was a bit daunting in the big running sea but the waves were regular and all fairly similar in size. We settled down to a slow but steady paddle north. Very soon the first of the large rocky islets which give the loch its name (madadh being Gaelic for 'dog' or 'wolf'), appeared. We tried to slip between Madadh Gruamach and the mainland of North Uist but the sea was too confused and chaotic to pass safely through. Instead we veered off to the right to take the outside route. The next 'madadh', Madadh Mòr, is further offshore which meant the inside passage was less hazardous. We bounced through before turning west into Loch nam Madadh and shelter, pleased to have cracked it at last.

Bizarrely, I never seem to learn from situations such as these nor from increased local knowledge. Several years later, I was doing a day paddle by myself in Loch nam Madadh in a borrowed boat and came out to the mouth of the loch to be met with similar conditions. The wind was strong from the north-east and the sea was a good force 5–6. I thought I would head down to Loch Euphoirt as it wasn't too far and then scrounge a lift back afterwards. I had only gone a short distance and realised that the seas, bigger than I first thought, were testing my skills to the limit. Turning back would be tricky. The boat I had borrowed was empty and very high-bowed, making it difficult to bring it up into the wind. I decided to carry on. I was concerned that if I were trashed by the waves and didn't manage to roll up again I would very quickly end up on the rocks off to my right. The outcome – one broken boat and one very unhappy boat owner. I headed further out to sea to give myself some space and concentrated on keeping the boat's bow heading straight as it surfed down the face of each wave. The journey along the coast was certainly very quick and in no time I was off the mouth of Loch Euphoirt. The next worry was the state of the tide and the potential for an ebb tide running out of the loch and clashing with the big waves I was in. As luck would have it, the tide was flooding into the loch and the journey in was uneventful. I paddled up the loch to the top end, sat for an hour or two behind a wall in sunshine, warm in my bivvy bag, eating lunch, snoozing, and thanking my lucky stars that I was safe.

Paddling into the loch with the wind now on our backs, the 3 kilometres to the township of Lochmaddy was quickly covered. Too tired to carry on we set up camp in a field near the hotel. It was early afternoon and although we had only travelled half the distance of previous days we were well satisfied with what we had salvaged from poor weather conditions. The following day, if the weather permitted, we would cross the Sound of Harris. For now, our first task was to have a brew and sleep for the afternoon. We were physically drained. When we awoke later in the early evening neither of us could be bothered cooking. We strolled off to the hotel and had a delicious bar meal of haddock and chips followed by a couple of pints of beer. We discussed the next day's crossing of the sound of Harris and hoped that the wind would have subsided sufficiently for us to make the passage to Harris.

Getting out of my sleeping bag the following morning was mighty hard. Still tired from the previous day I kind of hoped for bad weather so that we could stop for a rest day. A quick squint out of the tent showed that conditions were fine and that Andrea was already up and getting ready to move on. Groan!

Once on the water I still felt tired and found the 3 kilometres to the north end of the mouth of the loch really hard going. Not so Andrea. She romped ahead with boundless energy. I finally caught up with her below the lighthouse at Rubha an Fhigheadair where we turned north to cover the last 4 kilometres of North Uist. At last we were escaping the influence of Eaval. The sea was much more settled than yesterday, the remnants of the previous day's rough seas slowly dying down. There was no wind and the paddling was easy.

The stretch of water at the southern side of the Sound of Harris is treacherous. A combination of rolling seas from the Atlantic colliding with the tides and reefs in the sound makes the passage for boats of all sizes hazardous. After a brief stop on a pebble spit on the west side of the island of Thernatraigh we aimed straight for Renish Point, south of the houses at Rodel on south-east Harris. As the morning wore on the sea became very flat and half way across the sound we were paddling on a glass-like surface. Better still, the sun came out. No other boat traffic came through the sound and the only activity we could see were two clam boats off to the east working their way systematically up and down a short stretch of the Minch. We reached the shores of Harris and stopped for lunch at the small hamlet of Rodel.

The harbour was initially a bit tricky to find and after one false entry into the wrong bay we managed to locate the anchorage. The tide was out as we pulled up below the crumbling stone wall of the pier. We dragged the boats up the seaweed-covered shore, past a series of discarded lumps of metal and broken bottles and tied them securely to a fence high up on the shore. On the grass by the pier was a collection of ramshackle buildings, piles of rotting fishing nets and abandoned cars in various states of decay. The place looked as though it had been abandoned decades before, its occupants having walked away as a result of some awful event.

The atmosphere of the place was quite simply depressing, creating a sense of gloom and foreboding. We couldn't put our finger on what it was about the place that gave us the heebie-jeebies, but whatever it was we were not keen to hang around for a moment longer than we had to. So, sandwiches eaten, we dragged the boats back down the slope, launched and headed off without a backwards glance, relieved to be gone from this malevolent corner. Earlier thoughts of going to see the church of St Clements which has a unique square section tower standing high above the harbour and built about 1,500 AD from sandstone imported from Mull, were quickly forgotten. In no time we were paddling away at a good lick. Ten minutes or so later we stopped for a breather and a chat about what we had experienced back in Rodel. Were we foolish to leave so impulsively? Never before or since has such a feeling of blackness about a place come over me.

The coast from here was indented with bays and was a joy to paddle along. Soon we entered the narrow channel which separates the mainland from the small island of Eilean Lingereabhagh. Once inside, the channel opened up to form a wonderful natural anchorage; the water was shallow and the seabed's white sand gave the place a tropical air. We stopped for a few minutes, drifting in the slight current, taking in the atmosphere of the surroundings. This was a part of Harris which I had read so much about but I had never been quite sure of its location. It was infamous for the proposed aggregates 'super quarry', which, if allowed to go ahead would see the removal of the entire hillside above us. Once the landscape has been destroyed it can never be brought back and the scar would be there for evermore. I took some photographs of the bay and hill to remind me of a beautiful corner of Harris, just in case ...

It was now after 2 o'clock and time to push on for another couple of hours' paddling before finding a campsite. The coast was peppered with little inlets and tidal rapids and on the hill above we could occasionally make out the small single-track road picking its way along the south side of the island. It is known locally as the Golden Road, a reflection on the cost of building it. We did not hurry along and took some time to explore some of the inlets. On the map we noticed two tidal lagoons on the north side of Manish peninsula a few kilometres to the east of us. These might offer some potential for a campsite, we thought. A tidal lagoon in this area is known by its Gaelic name, *ob*. An *ob* occurs when small sea lochs are almost pinched off from the outer sea by a narrow entrance which often dries at low tide, leaving a pocket of water stranded until the sea's return on the next flood tide. As a consequence of this unusual tidal regime, the marine life is quite different from that in the surrounding sea. The discovery in such tidal lagoons of creatures not normally found in shallow water is a non-diving marine biologist's heaven.

We rounded the headland at Manish and headed for the first channel to try to access Ob Scalla, but this didn't work, as the channel was too shallow and there was rock strewn about. A few hundred metres to the north the map showed the next channel of Ob Leasaid, but try as we might, we could not locate it from the sea. After searching for ten minutes or so, a small creel boat motored round the headland, passed us in a wide arc and headed straight for the rocky coast, then vanished behind a small rocky promontory. Bingo! We followed it in and came across the narrow entrance to the channel which was only 2–3 metres across but ran for half a kilometre before opening out into a superb natural harbour. We slid in on the now rising tide and set up camp by the edge of the channel on top of a couple of old lazy beds as these provided the only dry land. The term 'lazy beds' describes the working of the thin soil from days before the Clearances. Crofters and their families worked hard to improve the soil fertility using kelp as fertilizer, turning it into long raised strips that had enough depth to grow subsistence crops such as potatoes. The name for these hard-won pieces of arable land is rather ironic considering the effort put into them. The entire length of the west coast of Scotland and many of the islands are lined with abandoned lazy beds and old farmsteads, a sad reminder to us of the people who lived in these places not so long ago.

Despite the relatively easy paddle we were tired and soon settled into our tents to read and complete diary entries for the day. The night was calm and I slept soundly until 7 a.m. the following morning.

The morning was rather dull, a bit damp, and breezy. We broke camp and paddled back out of Ob Leasaid into a freshening sea.Travelling along the south-east coast of Harris we were very exposed to southerly winds. Should the seas grow too large to cope with, the coast, indented with sea lochs, would afford shelter. I found the first hour or two hard going and struggled to keep up with Andrea. In quick succession we passed Loch Geocrab, Loch Stocinis, Loch Chliuthair, Loch Greosabhagh and then, after 8 kilometres, we rounded the headland of Reibinis to turn north towards Tarbert. The wind was gaining strength and the waves were bashing into our right-hand sides giving the occasional dousing in spray. Tarbert lay another 8 kilometres to the north and we were already tempted to make this the final destination for the day as the weather was steadily deteriorating. When we turned north we had the sea on our backs and the waves and wind carried us quickly up past the many islets which pockmark the entrance to Loch Tarbert. I was quite chilled at this point and despite the speed of our progress in the following sea, I was looking forward to arriving at Tarbert, a tea-room and warmth. As we approached the harbour, the CalMac ferry appeared off our right shoulders. We hadn't heard it approaching over the noise of the wind and sea. It sped past, some 100 metres away, still going flat-out.

As we followed the ferry into the harbour at Tarbert the rain began and our spirits dropped a notch. Ten minutes later we stood damp and dripping on a concrete slip. There was no point in changing into dry clothes as they too would have been soaked in next to no time. We set off to the tearoom in our dripping canoeing clobber. Conversation was non-existent: we were both lost in our own thoughts. What were we doing here in such miserable conditions? Was this really a holiday? How could we retrieve the situation? Should we just go home?

In the village square we found a teashop and squelched in. It was full of holidaymakers, all dry and warm. The owner guided us to the table by the open log fire. Despite apologising for our general soggy decrepitude we were made to feel very welcome indeed. We sat in the corner and dripped (this was becoming a recurring theme) as we supped hot coffee and dined on fried egg rolls and carrot cake. Perfect. The heat of the small tearoom eventually warmed us through and the thought of leaving to set off in the boats again was not appealing. The other holidaymakers drifted off, more than likely to drive to their comfortable B&Bs. As the tearoom owner cleared the tables we learned that there was not much chance of finding a good camping spot locally. A privately owned hostel at Rhenigidale was probably our only option for a warm dry night. This was some distance further on but the thought of its comfort was very appealing. If only we could get there in the worsening conditions outside. The rain was now beating off the windows and the world looked very miserable indeed.

Then came a surprise. The owner said that the tea-room had a floored attic which we could use for the night if we wished. What a dilemma: to paddle on to try and make the hostel or stay put having only paddled 18 kilometres that morning. After a lot of debate and delay we opted for pushing on to reach the hostel which lay 12 kilometres further on up the coast. We did not know if it would even have spaces for us and for some reason it didn't occur to us to phone ahead to ask. We thanked the tearoom owner profusely before braving the elements again and launching the boats back into the windy grey East Loch Tarbert.

For the next 5 kilometres we had to run south-east to gain the shelter of the large island of Scalpay. This meant a slog more or less straight into the prevailing weather and rough sea. It was absolute torture trying to make headway into the howling wind. As happened on a previous trip round Skye, every time the paddles were raised into the air the wind caught the blades to twist them from our grasps. This really was hard going and after an hour of paddling we were nowhere near the shelter of Scalpay. In contrast to her strength of the previous day, Andrea was now becoming exhausted and her forward progress grew slower and slower. Twice we discussed turning back and stopping at Tarbert for the night but as we only had such a short way to go until we would have shelter from the island, we carried on. Forty minutes later, we made the entrance of the Sound of Scalpay and gained some relief from the wind. The sound is only about 200 metres wide and is now crossed by an elegant, toll-free bridge, creating scenery reminiscent of Norway.

The island of Scalpay is unusual for this part of the world it that it is fairly populous. Whilst the other satellite islands in the Western Isles suffered severe depopulation over the last hundred or so years, Scalpay's population has remained fairly stable. Its people make a living from fishing and woollen hand-knitted garments. More recently a large fish-processing factory has been built to take farmed salmon from the many cages in the area. I wondered what contributed to this island's relative prosperity.

Under the bridge we stopped briefly at the old ferry slip. Another 2 kilometres would see us back out from behind the island and in the full force of the weather again. Having come this far there was no talk of turning back. Sure enough, as we emerged from the shelter of the sound we were hit by fierce winds and a growing sea. Fortunately, the hostel was now only 3.5 kilometres north and at least when we turned left the sea and wind were on our backs pushing us straight towards the little bay below the hostel. In only thirty minutes or so we had covered the distance, surfing down the face of the waves in great style. Eager to finish for the day, our spirits were at last beginning to lift. Nevertheless, being a worrier, I was becoming increasingly concerned about the landing on the stony foreshore in such a large sea. As we approached the bay we back-paddled up the faces of a few sets of waves to slow down and stall our forward progress enough to assess the landing.

There was quite a bit of refraction either side of the bay, which was only some 50 metres across, but in the centre there was an obvious route in, where the waves ran straight on to the shore in a series of dumping explosions. Waiting for a bigger set of waves to pass under us, I set off first to see how it would go, and to help Andrea in once I had landed – assuming that I didn't totally botch that up. By luck more than skill, I caught one of the smaller waves perfectly, riding just behind its peak to land fairly easily on the stones as it broke onto the shore. Scrambling out of the boat was as usual hazardous in such conditions and as ever I got soaked in the seconds it took to haul off the spraydeck and slip out of the cockpit. Once I had dragged the boat a few metres up the shore I ran back to watch Andrea come in; she timed it perfectly and as soon as the bow touched the shore I grabbed it, hauling the boat free of the breaking surf. Wow! Were we elated? Despite being cold, wet and very tired, we hollered and whooped round the beach in a mad, triumphant dance, so very pleased and relieved to be safely ashore. Little did we know that two of the hostel's occupants were watching out of the front window above us – not that it would have bothered us much at that moment.

Once we had secured the boats and changed into dry clothes we wandered up the grass at the back of the bay to see if there was room at the hostel. The thought of setting up camp was not all that appealing. The hostel was a small stone built house and when we popped our heads into the main room we found two other residents. Our luck was in. There were plenty of bunks, plus, joy of joys, a hot shower.

Rhenigidale Hostel is one of four private hostels in the Western Isles, owned by the Gatliff Trust (Urras Osdailean Nan Innse Gall Gatliff), a 'not for profit' voluntary organisation with charitable status, working with islanders to establish and maintain a chain of Crofters' Hostels to sound basic standard throughout the Hebrides. The hostel was wardened from its opening in 1962 until his death by Roddy McInnes. Roddy was a character, described as irrepressible and indomitable. He was a man of few words who could, nevertheless, spare a few minutes for every hosteller. While Roddy's ways never changed, death did bring change, change Roddy would have approved. Until recent years there had been no road to the hostel and all land access was via a long path from the end of the public road east of Tarbert. On 20th February 1990 the road to Rhenigdale arrived, 8 kilometres of tarmac winding over the watershed from a road junction at Maaruig on the main Stornoway road. Even with the road the hostel is still very isolated, but very welcoming.

We decided to stay for two nights as we needed the chance to rest and sort out our sodden gear. The next day the wind was forecast to continue from the south-east. In all probability paddling would be hard going: all the more reason to hole up. Once sorted out and showered we introduced ourselves to the hostel's occupants. Our companions for the evening were from Australia and were making their way round Scotland bit by bit, in no particular hurry. They planned to move on the next day by car and make for Stornoway. They had spent the afternoon in the hostel to avoid the rain and wind and had got the wood-burning stove going full tilt so that the small room was oozing heat. This was ideal for our kayaking gear and soon we had it hung up above the fireplace on a string, drips hissing as they dropped onto the hot stove. As the girls had watched us arrive and had been ready to rush to our assistance if we had been trashed on the shore, they were relieved to see us land safely. After dinner another soaked man, a Dutch student, joined our small group and we spent a very pleasant evening chatting about everything and nothing. Later, when I hit my bunk for the night, the rain and wind were still battering on the slates above my head but I was happy – warm and tired – and entered the land of nod in seconds.

I awoke late the next morning and when finally I descended, the others were busy preparing for the day. The weather was very overcast and heavy, although the rain had lessened to a fine drizzle and the wind had dropped. Neither Andrea nor myself wished to stay in the hostel throughout the day. While it might have been good to sit and read the books I had brought, we instead set off to climb the nearby hill of Clisham, which at 799 metres, is the highest hill in the Western Isles. We scrounged a lift along the road from the girls and jammed ourselves in the back of their hired Micra, crammed between their mass of unpacked clutter. Luckily the journey was short. As I couldn't see anything but the roof lining of the vehicle I felt car-sick.

The hill was straightforward, except that from the point we left the road and took to the slopes the cloud was so low that we saw nothing for the entire walk. We traipsed through streams of water running over the surface of the peat and grassy slopes. The rain came down and within minutes we were soaked – again! We persevered, using a compass to steer us through the murk to the top, only to slip and slither back down the hill to the road. As it was only midday and too early to retire to the hostel we set our sights on the highlights of Tarbert, some 9 kilometres away, once again. Having hitched lifts many times before we felt sure that we would land lucky. Two hours later, drenched and very dejected, we walked into Tarbert.

I suppose I wouldn't have stopped for us either! Our only consolation was the warmth of the tearoom again and creating puddles on the floor once more. Refreshed by a superb coffee, scone and jam, we delayed leaving for as long as possible. Our first thoughts were to walk back over the old access route to the hostel but as we paid our bill the owner said that there would be a bus leaving for the hostel in ten minutes. There was no need to hesitate: we sped across the square to make sure we didn't miss it. Also on the bus was one of the Gatliff Trust organisers arriving for a meeting with the warden the next day.

Once back in the hostel we embarked again on the ritual of drying out and endless cups of hot tea. At last I had a chance to read the latest copy of the newspaper that we had bought in Tarbert and apart from chatting to the Dutch lad I recall little of that evening. I slipped off to bed early and hoped to high heaven that the following day would bring better weather.

The next morning I awoke early to absolute silence! This was strange. I crawled out of my sleeping bag to wipe the condensation off the skylight window and peer out across the landscape. The sun wasn't up yet and there were a few whisps of mist dotted across the damp glen, but as far as I could make out, the sky was clear and the branches on the scraggy birch trees across the field were still. Early morning can be magical, the weather not having made up its mind on what it might do for the day, leaving the world in anticipation of what might unfold. In the same attic room was the man from the Gatcliff Trust, still asleep. With as little noise as possible I packed my gear into the waterproof sacks and carried it downstairs. Andrea was already in the kitchen eating breakfast and preparing to set off. In the quiet of the hostel, we hardly said a word as we packed and pulled our slightly salt-impregnated, stiff, dry garments off the string over the stove. We dared not say that the weather looked promising in case the spell would be broken and the wind and rain would return.

Several journeys to and from the kayaks later we were ready and, making sure that our buoyancy aids had enough snack bars and a full water pouch for the day ahead, we carried the boats into the water. As we launched, our Dutch hostel companion appeared to bid us farewell and good luck with the weather and the rest of the voyage. He was toting his camera and with the sun making its first dim appearance on the horizon he ushered us into correct positions for some photos of the boats and us against the brightening sky. Finally we turned our bows east and set off, shouting our farewells and giving a last wave to the paparazzi.

We had now both fully recovered from our exertions and were looking forward to the day ahead. Within minutes we had left the bay behind and were crossing the mouth of Loch Seaforth. This is one of the most impressive of the sea lochs of the Western Isles, its sides forming a classic glaciated U-shaped valley which reminded me of my school geography-book diagrams. It runs for 25 kilometres into the interior of

Harris and must once have been an important anchorage for our Viking compatriots in an earlier age. The sea was mirror-calm and the paddling was magical; the boats slipped through the water effortlessly. This ease of the first kilometre or two was distinctly odd as most mornings when you set off the boats feel heavy and lethargic and getting into stride can take a while.

We knew that two more good days of fine weather would allow us to complete our planned route and reach the 'big smoke' of Stornoway. As we exchanged the occasional comment on the scenery or weather we were both conscious that time was running out and that a voyage such as this does not allow for sustained enjoyment of the peace and tranquillity of places we pass.

Once across Loch Seaforth and then past the mouth of its sister, Loch Claidh, we rounded the headland of Gob Rubha Bhalamuis Bhig to see, off our starboard bows, the distinctive outline of the Shiant Islands only 9 kilometres ahead of us. The high northern cliffs of Garbh Eilean were a dominant feature. The Shiants are a fascinating small group of islands, one of whose protected residents is the black (plague) rat, *Rattus rattus*, which first arrived here from a shipwreck. One of the island's previous owners, the author Sir Compton MacKenzie, tried to rid the place of them by importing cats, but they soon perished. A more sinister characteristic is that the local seas are reputed to be inhabited by the ghostly Blue Men of the Minch to whom you must only speak Gaelic if you wish to remain in this world. In the late 19th century, the Rev. John Campbell, claimed that one followed his boat; 'a blue-covered man, with a long, grey face, and floating from the waist out of the water' – sounds more like a sinking sea kayaker! Of less dramatic interest are vast columnar basaltic columns rising up the cliffs on the north side, similar to those found on Staffa but many times the height. The current owner of the islands, Adam Nicolson, has written a marvellous account of the islands which fuelled my desire to visit them (*Sea Room: An Island Life in the Hebrides*, Harper Collins, 2001).

The lure of the Shiants was strong but as Andrea and I had to return to work on Monday there would be no time to explore the islands on this occasion. We would return soon, we thought, and perhaps spot a black rat or two. I was reminded of a book on Mongolia which I had recently read, which described numerous recurring outbreaks of bubonic plague caused by locals eating marmot that had been sickly when killed. Each time an outbreak occurred the authorities closed off all roads out of the village or region of steppe until the illness passed.

The waters between the Shiants and Harris are very treacherous. A ridge of rocks runs between the point at Rubha Uisinis and the islands which forces the deep waters of the Minch over the top, creating fearsome tidal overfalls, similar to the rapids in a river. The extreme nature of this passage, when the wind is against the tide, creates dangerous conditions which no doubt give rise to the legends of the Blue Men.

For the next 7 kilometres we paddled on, enjoying the morning light and increasing warmth from the rising sun. For the first time on this trip we dug out sunglasses from our buoyancy aid front pockets, washed off the biscuit crumbs, and felt a bit like poseurs on some exotic foreign expedition – grinning at each other in the fantastic conditions.

We paddled up the coast, enjoying the flat sea and the chance to potter in and out of rocky inlets and bays, stopping to chat and point out items of interest and generally holding off finishing our trip. By midday we arrived at the bay of Mol Truisg, pulled the boats up the slippery cobbles and stopped for lunch. We found a blue fish box to use as a table and laid out our spread: tuna mayonnaise sandwiches, cherry tomatoes and black tea. The sun was now at its highest and we basked in its warmth, soaking up every therm in the knowledge that it was now nearing the end of the summer. Every day of sunshine could now count as a bonus before shortened autumn days and winter set in. I am of the opinion that even in the latitudes of northern Scotland long winters of limited daylight and little sunshine have a profound influence on inhabitants' moods. No sun definitely makes Jack a dull boy.

After much delay we eventually packed up and returned to the boats which had been left high and dry by the falling tide. The large smooth tide-exposed boulders were covered in slime and extremely difficult to negotiate whilst carrying the kayaks to the water. Several agonising bumps and thumps later we reached the sea and set off again to the north. Within minutes, against all rules and safety sense, we discarded our buoyancy aids, stuffing them under the deck lines in front of us; we were too hot in the afternoon sun. The next 17 kilometres to our campsite were once again a blur. We paddled some distance apart, both lost in our own worlds, Andrea picking her way round the coast, stopping every now and then to examine marine life exposed by the low tide. I opted to stay offshore and simply lollop along at an easy pace, enjoying being in such a marvellous place. Looking at the map as I write this, I realise that the sea lochs and bays we passed must have been of considerable interest but we slipped past, content in our own private worlds. This was almost defensive. The end of the trip in sight, I had distanced myself from my surroundings and retreated into myself to eke out every last moment of happiness. Somehow, visiting a village in one of the lochs or meeting a passing fishing boat would have destroyed the experience.

By late afternoon we realised that we were within easy striking distance of Stornoway. We should stop for the day as finding a decent spot to camp nearer the town might not be possible. We pulled in to the clutter of islets off Mharbhig and found a likely location just south of the hamlet of Cromor. The only spot to set up our tents was a soggy green patch of ground that once held a series of lazy beds above the high water mark. Picking the highest of the lazy beds we pitched the tents, one above the other. The soggy ooze below the tent permeated the groundsheet so that each time I moved, the ground squelched below. As there was no other obvious place to camp we stayed put. We pooled food remants for dinner: dried potatoes, beans and quorn sausages. Satisfied, we clambered up onto a rocky outcrop above our boggy campsite. Drinking tea and content with the day's paddling, we noticed a man below us skirting the tide line with a purposeful air about him, carrying a gun or rifle under his arm. Passing our kayaks, which were lying on the high foreshore, he clambered into a small dingy and rowed off into the dusk. We had gone very quiet as he passed but now we discussed what on earth he might be up to. He would have been aware of our presence as our kayaks and tents were brightly coloured and fairly obvious. Shortly afterwards we retired. The following morning we would paddle into Stornoway, the end of a memorable holiday.

Morning came all too soon: our last day. The skies were grey and the wind was again brisk but had veered to the south. We dithered over breakfast, in no hurry to paddle the last few kilometres.

Stornoway harbour heralded the end. We both had work commitments: Andrea stayed on the island and I took both kayaks by ferry back to Ullapool.

Because of the varied weather kayaking had had its wet and uneasy moments but I would not have missed it for anything. Whilst it could not count as a major paddling achievement, it was a trip that required us to commit to the paddle and not opt out when the weather deteriorated.

Before we parted, the plans for the next trip from Loch Boisdale south were already hatched.

Best meal on trip: bean tagine

Olive oil
1 onion, chopped
2 cloves garlic, crushed
2 spring onions, finely chopped
1 can of beans (haricot, lima or butter)

2–3 teaspoons paprika
1 teaspoon cumin
1 chilli, deseeded and chopped
Tomato purée
1 can chopped tomatoes
(spinach if possible)

Fry the onion, garlic and spring onions until soft. Add the beans, some water (or vegetable stock) and bring to the boil. Add the chilli, tomatoes and tomato purée. Simmer for 15 minutes. The flavours in this dish improve if left to stand. Serve with bread and red wine.

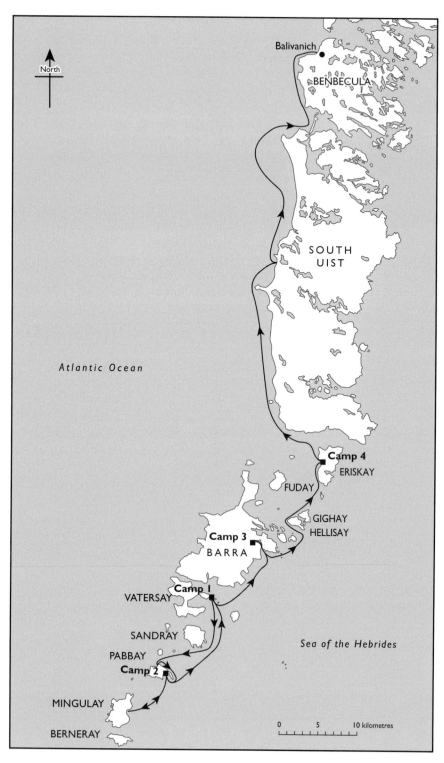

Chapter 4

Barra, Mingulay and Rapier Missiles

The trip from Loch Boisdale to Stornoway whetted our appetites for the Western Isles and after pouring over maps during long winter nights, Andrea and I plumped for an excursion to Mingulay, Barra and South Uist, albeit with some trepidation. Psychologically, Mingulay was a biggy, not because of distance but because the area is exposed in bad weather with large seas running in from the Atlantic. As soon as sea-kayaking friends heard of our plans, tales of horrendous seas and near disasters rang in our ears. There were stories of people forced to hole up in tents when the weather changed and Atlantic lows landed, waiting for a couple of days for the sea to calm down.

In addition to Andrea and myself, a friend, Graham Anderson, was to accompany us for part of the journey before re-joining his wife and daughter who were travelling with us to the Western Isles. Graham was a rock-solid paddler, having spent several years on Shetland, and we were glad to have him along.

With three kayaks plus two bikes carefully jammed on top of his car, Graham drove gingerly on to the ferry's car deck, petrified that the whole lot would fall off as he boarded. Once on board, we untied the kayaks and laid them on the decks – many pounds saved! It's great to be a mean Scotsman! Also on board the ferry were three double kayaks, trussed up against the sides of the car deck. Where were they off to?

The crossing was flat calm, an encouraging sign for the paddling to come. As young Eilidh was soon bored by Postman Pat books and card tricks we sent her off to fetch some drinking straws. Before long we had twisted and tied them into arctic explorers pulling sleds, Inuits in kayaks hunting seals and, a procession of giraffes striding across the plains (with blue and red spiral legs). Even with such distractions the journey across the Minch was tediously long and Graham teased Andrea who had paddled across the Minch with her partner some years before. Lochmaddy to Uig – was it worth the saving of the ferry fare?

As the ferry neared Castlebay I stood on the deck looking out for a place to camp. We had reckoned from the map that we should paddle south across the bay to some sheltered beaches on Vatersay for the first night's camping. While I peered across the water, one of the party who owned the double kayaks suggested that the best place for us to camp was close by the slip. When the ferry docked both sea-kayak parties ended up on the same small concrete slip nearby. The other party, having nipped in first, dumped their boats at the bottom of the slip, blocking it for us. Although our boats were already packed and all we had to do was to don our personal kayaking kit, spraydecks and buoyancy aids, the others wouldn't budge to let us past. We stood back and let them pack in their own time.

Eventually the other party were set, launched, then took off with a vengeance – due south, towards Vatersay! We paddled behind them, bemused as they had recommended the campsite close to the pier. We chose the smaller of the two bays on Vatersay, and, in almost total darkness, beached, then set up camp on the sand dunes ready for some well-earned sleep.

In the wee early hours the wind got up and the tents shook and flapped quite worryingly, forcing me to get up twice. I pegged the guy lines and later checked that our boats and paddles were secure behind a sand dune. By morning the weather was not at all good. We lay in our sleeping bags trying to snooze and ignore the conditions outside but to no avail. One by one we emerged and lit the stove for the first brew of the day. The sea off to the right of the headland was being whipped up into a white-tipped frenzy. With the wind coming from the south-east the waves were not very high despite the frantic nature of wind. However, the forecast affirmed our worst fears: 'Hebrides, south-east, force 6–7, imminent'. Too right it was.

This was only the first day of the trip and we were eager to get going. Nevertheless, it was a real pleasure to sneak back into our warm sleeping bags for some blissful sleep. Later, we surfaced again for a second breakfast. The rain came in sporadic showers confining us to our separate tents while we carried out chores, communicating by shouting across to each other above the noise of the wind. Later in the morning I sauntered over to the kayakers we encountered the previous evening to see what they were planning. They were confident that they would set off soon as their double kayaks could easily cope with the sea as it was. Our single kayaks could have coped as well, we thought, but considering the very exposed nature of this part of the Western Isles we knew that getting into difficulties could be fatal. Just after lunch two of the doubles set off past our camp and headed south round the headland, straight into the waves. Within seconds one turned back and the other reappeared some ten minutes later. That was it for the day! The only signs of life were from the wisps of smoke from the campfire they had lit from old wooden pallets gleaned from the beach.

Suffering from 'cabin fever' I asked Andrea if I could have a shot of her kayak, a shiny new Nordkapp Jubilee. I had been thinking of getting a similar one and was keen to see how it felt in a lumpy sea. For half an hour or so I pottered around in the waves off the headland, enjoying the feel of the boat and its responsiveness in the sea. The only problem I could find with it was that the high bow caught the wind. This made it a swine to turn unless it was canted right over on its edge to lower the windage and make the turn easier. When I got back it turned out that the stern hold was full of Andrea's food for the week making the back end of the boat heavy in the water. This explained the poor turning-ability. Back at the camp, we dug out the playing cards and whiled away the rest of the day with Gin Rummy and Knockout Whist.

By early evening we had eaten and were prepared for the following day. The forecast was promising and our hopes were high. Annoyingly, alcohol-induced singing from the camp next door kept us awake for part of the night.

From our campsite on Vatersay the distance to the top end of Mingulay was only 12 kilometres, a short paddle in anyone's book. We did not savour the idea of being stranded on Mingulay waiting for the seas to subside as time was of the essence, but, should that happen, the sooner we set off the better. With fingers crossed, we left the camp by 8 a.m. As we pulled out, the doubles group were making final preparations to depart. It would only take an hour to reach the next island of Sandray. The seas were still pretty bouncy from the previous day's poor weather but at least the wind was down to a gentle breeze. Spirits were high as we were paddling at last.

This was Graham's first outing in his new boat, a Pintail from Valley Canoe Products. He had sold his older version of the same boat to buy this new one. Whilst he had assumed it would be exactly the same as its predecessor, it turned out that the hull shape had been modified. It took some time for him to get the hang of this but to this day he wishes he had kept his old boat.

After a quick, post-breakfast, coffee-induced stop on the south-east-facing beach on Sandray we decided to head south-west across the channel of Caolas Phabaigh to skirt down the west side of Pabbay, the next island in the chain before turning due south for Mingulay. The seas were rising a few notches as we entered the channel. For once we had done some very careful tidal calculations and knew that there was a tide running from east to west at this time. As we would be going the same direction as the tide, the rising sea should not pose too much hardship. Of some concern was that the three of us were spaced out over several hundred metres and I could only see the others on odd occasions when we happened to be on the crests of waves simultaneously.

In very quick time we had shot across the 5 kilometres of the channel and were bearing down on the high cliffs at the north end of Pabbay. At this point Andrea and I ended up side by side; Graham was a little way behind. A short distance in front of us we could discern a subtle change in the shapes and colour of the waves. There was a definite line of white-topped waves running from the northwest corner of the island, rising almost as a solid wall northwards across the channel. We then came across some rafts of puffins and guillemots. A few moments later the seabirds increased in number and it occurred to me that they were feeding on the edge of the now clearly obvious turbulent seas in front of us. The current that was carrying us westwards was running bang into the westerly swell coming in from the Atlantic. I was instantly alarmed at the fast developing situation. There was no place to land on the west side of Pabbay, even if we did punch our way through the line of turbulent waves and then the open ocean swell. We were in trouble.

A few frantic moments of calling to each other and Andrea and I decided to turn back, pick up Graham who was now approaching, and head as fast as we could paddle back to the east side of Pabbay. The first few minutes of the return paddle were extremely hard work. With half an eye on the cliffs to our right I could see that we were not making any headway against the current. The others were also paddling like fury and progress was not happening. We tried moving sideways towards the cliff base in an attempt to edge out of the main channel and hopefully also out of the stronger part of the current. This was a slightly risky move, as the seas were breaking up the face of the cliffs in spectacular explosions. We were clearly between the devil and a hard place. A long exhausting paddle eventually pulled us out of the worst of the current and the big seas. By the time we arrived at the north-east side of Pabbay the sun had come out and the waves had dropped to a mere bouncy chop. The contrast was amazing.

We wondered if the seas were still big back at the point where we turned around. In a way we felt as if we had wimped out of the west coast but at the same time we were glad to have done so. My heart was still thumping as we discussed the next plan of action. Andrea was a bit shattered from the hard paddle, both mentally and physically. We towed her into the beautiful beach at Bàgh Bàn. Though still early in the day we stopped for lunch and to relax. The bay was sheltered and backed by large grass-topped sand dunes which would make a perfect campsite. We earmarked a site in case we passed by again. Sitting in the sun we wondered what had become of the paddlers in the doubles. They would have left shortly after us and were to take the same route to Mingulay. We should have seen them by now, as double kayaks are fast boats and very seaworthy. Our VHF radios were turned on for safety in case either the others, or ourselves, required help.

From our beach on Pabbay, the paddle to Mingulay was only 4 kilometres. Following a lengthy break we set off down the east side of the island. Once out again into the next channel between Pabbay and Mingulay large seas were still lumping in from the west. The tide had turned by now which meant that it would not clash with the high seas. Graham was also happier as for the first time that day he could stop and roll up his cigarettes by himself without having to get one of us to raft up to him to provide support during this tricky operation.

The crossing to Mingulay was very enjoyable and we soon pulled into the shelter of the sea stacks of Solon Mòr and Solon Beag (the big and little gannets) that stood so grandly off the island's northerly headland. From this angle we could see the east-to-west shape of the island. The west coast has high precipitous cliffs much favoured by climbers. The land then runs quickly down to the low-lying east and southern coasts where the islanders had subsisted for about 2,000 years on fishing, seabirds and crofting until the departure of the last inhabitants in 1912. Although not as far from civilisation as the more remote islands of St. Kilda, Mingulay has many parallels. For many months at a time the small community would have been cut off from the rest of the world by the elements. Survival often depended on the harvesting of seabirds. Their rent to the landowner partly consisted of shearwater chicks collected, St. Kilda-style, from the cliff tops on the west side. In more recent times the island has only been used to graze sheep. Sadly, the village houses above the dunes of Mingulay Bay are falling into disrepair and it seems unlikely that there will ever be permanent human habitation again on the island.

We approached the headland, just before the turn into the beach and stopped paddling for a few minutes to watch the cruise ship, *Hebridean Princess*, pull out of the bay and pass us not many metres away. My thoughts returned to a visit to St Kilda a few years previously on a diving trip. There too a cruise liner made a brief stop-over. We knew the zodiac pilot, Barbara Jones, and helped her assist her older, mainly Italian and American, charges ashore so that they could make the short walk to the NAAFI shop for their postcards and special St Kildan stamps.

We paddled lazily into the bay and towards the long sandy beach, upon which a group of ten or so seals lay dozing, watching our approach out of the corners of their half-closed eyes. Only when we were very close to land did they finally wobble into the water. The sea was still bumpy, even on the sheltered side of the island, and embarrassingly I fluffed my final approach. The stern caught on a breaking wave, sweeping the boat suddenly sideways into a classic broach. I braced frantically but with no effect before being dumped ignominiously on the sand in a froth of foam and receding water. Soaked and sand engrained, I sorted myself out and dragged my boat up the beach to watch the other two come in behind me. This they did with sublime skill, hopping out of their boats, bone dry, with ease onto sand. Huh, show-offs! The seals bobbed offshore, watching us for a few minutes, then hauled themselves back out further along the beach to enjoy some more sunshine and resume their forty winks in peace.

As we walked up to the old village we were keenly aware of how special the place was. We could appreciate the struggle for survival that must have been the norm for the islanders on land that was now poor and only fit for rough grazing. Even that seemed to be in short supply and not enough to support the population of more than a hundred who once lived here. The only other place where I have felt such a palpable connection with the past was on Hirta, the main island of St Kilda. As we wandered about the old houses I wondered if the expectation of life of its former inhabitants was perhaps lower than in other islands, one which was purely of survival against the elements and limited resources. However, the sea at the time would have provided a rich harvest of fish, shellfish and kelp on their doorstep.

The only other people on the island were climbers who had been dropped off the previous day from a chartered fishing boat. They had had a miserable crossing and were not looking forward to the return passage at the end of the week. Although we had originally planned to stay on the island overnight we decided to take our leave and return to Pabbay which promised better camping. By staying on Pabbay we would avoid the risk of being trapped on Mingulay if the weather deteriorated again. A previous visitor to the island, in days before the Clearances, was the factor for the estate who was put ashore to collect the rents for the year only to discover that the entire population had perished from some unknown disease. On returning to his compatriots in the awaiting boat with the news, they took fright and abandoned the poor man to his fate, not returning until a year later to collect him.

The short return passage to Pabbay was quickly covered and we dragged the boats up above the high-water mark just below the steep shell sand dunes, being careful not to squish any of the vast number of enormous brightly coloured snails that seemed to be the island's main residents. To the south of our landing point we could see the drag marks of kayaks running up the foreshore and could just see the tips of some sea kayaks poking out from behind the sand dunes. Aha! Our other paddling colleagues from the ferry? Camp was quickly set up on top of our dune and the first coffee of the stay brewed was in our 'proper coffee' Lakeland Plastics mugs, complete with their inbuilt coffee-grind strainers. Luxury!

We wandered over to our neighbours a few hundred yards away as they pottered around their tents. To our surprise the four guys weren't our previous companions at all but a bunch of naval-yard workers from Barrow in Furness. The oldest who was at least sixty recently had had both hips replaced. Surprisingly, they hadn't seen the other party of paddlers at all. They invited us to join them for drinks later. After our meal we could see smoke rising from the chimney in the gable end of the island's only house which stood in ruins on the hillside above the campsites. We extracted a bottle of wine from one of the boats and ambled over to chew the cud with them for a while.

In the fading evening light we swapped stories of kayaking stupidity and disasters. John, with the new hips, the elder statesman of the group, was a story teller supreme and had us captivated by a series of graphically-told adventures. One such was about the time he was paddling down Loch Morar, a freshwater loch near Mallaig, on his way to the isthmus just east of Swordland, planning to portage his kayak over to Tarbet, and on the next day to carry on down to Sourlies bothy at the head of Loch Nevis. It was late in the evening and the sun was low in the sky over Eigg behind him. Coming fast up the loch was a speedboat heading straight towards him. John realised that the speedboat driver was probably finding it hard to see properly with the setting sun in his eyes and almost certainly wouldn't see a kayak coming head-on towards him in the glare. John turned and made a run for the shore to avoid collision. When the speedboat was almost upon him, John dropped his paddle and dived into the water head first to capsize himself. Moments later the speedboat hit the upturned kayak hull just aft of the cockpit and crashed right over the top. John baled out and thankfully the startled speedboat driver turned his craft around to assist. This story was told with great aplomb and peppered with colourful language. I suspect the speedboat driver received an absolute rollocking for his lack of care.

We sat in a semi-circle well into the night, enjoying the easy company of the other group, the youngest lad tending the smokey fire with any scraps of flotsam that could be gleaned from the drift line below the sand dunes. They were in no hurry to move on and intended to stay a few days on Pabbay, doing – absolutely nothing. We planned to paddle on the next day, so, with a final toast to our hosts we called it a night and turned to our tents. Even with the crek-crek-creking of a corncrake somewhere up the hill behind us, we were not disturbed from our deep sleep.

We were up and off the next morning early. There was no movement from the other camp. The weather had improved a little: the sun was out and through the night the wind had veered round to the south-east. This would give us a helpful shove as we ran north again up to Castlebay where Graham was to rejoin his family for the rest of the week. Andrea and I planned to paddle on north.

Kayaking up the chain of islands to Barra was a pleasure. The following sea, although growing in size in the fresh wind, was perfect for surfing and we soon scooted across to the west side of Sandray and tucked into the lee of the land on the north side for a snack. High on the foreshore to our right was a single kayak. We couldn't see a tent or any signs of movement. As it was still early we assumed that its occupant must be around somewhere. We debated whether it could be one of the 'doubles' group. Certainly no-one from last night's Pabbay party was up and about. Perhaps we should have investigated.

The final crossings back to Vatersay and then Castlebay were quickly covered. We stopped for our second break next to Kisimul Castle that sits offshore from Castlebay on a rocky outcrop of land, giving the otherwise drab location a touch of grandeur. This imposing fortification of a castle, keep and grand hall was built in the 15th century and is the ancestral home of the MacNeil clan. The current chief is an American who visits regularly but the castle is open to the public on certain days of the week.

Graham had phoned Jane from Sandray and we could see her car drawing to a halt a short distance away on the sea front. We finished taking pictures of each other with the castle as a backdrop and then paddled over to join her and Eilidh. Jane had come down from Loch Boisdale earlier and was already settled in at the local hostel. We helped Graham to get organised, had lunch in the local café, and then said our farewells. We wanted to reach the north end of Barra before it was too late so that we could set up camp and organise our kit. We weren't very sure where we could find a camping spot as from the map the coast looked pretty rocky.

Once back out of the bay we turned east for a few kilometres, then north-east up the reef-strewn coast of the island. As we suspected, camping was not going to be possible and the couple of spots we tentatively approached were not to be. One feature on the map that intrigued me was the narrow channel just ahead of us, which we couldn't see until we were upon it, that led to the saline lagoon of Loch Ob. *Ob*, as explained in an earlier chapter on Uist, is a small west-coast tidal lagoon. The Gaelic word, derived from the Norwegian word 'hop', which means land-locked bay, has given rise to place names such as Oban. The tidal lagoon can vary in size from little more than a small swimming pool to many acres. The sills often become zones of very diverse marine life forced by the alternating tidal flow into shallow rapids, bringing food and nutrients to the area.

As we arrived at the point shown on the map where the entrance should be we almost paddled past the opening as it was so well hidden from view by other rocky outcrops and low cliffs that surrounded us. The channel in the rock was absolutely amazing. For a start it was as straight as a Roman road and the walls on either side looked as though they had been hewn by hand by a canal builder. It was hard to believe that this passage was natural and not man-made. The tide had been falling all afternoon and as we entered the passage we could see the sandy sea floor beneath the boats a few feet below. Paddling along the channel was fun as the walls were only a few feet away on each side and the water flow was running briskly against us. Half way along, the rock sill forced us to stop and drag the boats over a small waterfall into the upper part of the channel. Here the water was a little deeper and with less movement. Having paddled for over half a kilometre we emerged into the inland sea loch and as luck would have it, just to our left lay a series of old ruined croft houses surrounded by short sheep-grazed grass: the perfect camping spot.

This particular bit of land was surrounded by a fence with a gate. It was not until sometime later that we learned that it was an important archaelogical site which, of course, explained the fence. The old village of five or six former dwelling houses was called Buaile nam Bodach, 'meeting place of the old men'. The Buaile nam Bodach Preservation Society was set up in January 1999 to raise funds for archaeological research on the site. It is thought that there may also be a buried Viking village in the same area. Would crofters and Vikings have minded us setting up camp in their village? I doubt it. As it turned out, the best patch to make camp was inside the remains of one of the houses.

Dinner for the night was vegetable curry, rice and some rather bruised and battered nan bread dragged out of the far recesses of the boat. As we sat on the low wall next to the tent eating our meal, the wind dropped to nothing. That might have been pleasant indeed had it not immediately mustered the Barra midges who took off in their millions to seek their evening meal. Not wishing to be the main course on their menu, we retreated to the tent.

Once again through the night I had to nip outside to tension the tent and peg out the guy lines. In the morning we could tell that as it was pretty blowy here in the relative shelter of the *ob*, it would be many times worse out to sea. We spent a pleasant hour or so after breakfast paddling our empty boats round the *ob* before packing up the camp and setting off down the channel back to the sea. The tide was high enough to cover the rock sill and we had a quick uncomplicated paddle back out. The sea was pretty big and running obliquely on to the entrance to the channel. We went from flat calm boating-pond paddling one moment to hell-for-leather big sea waves the next. Even though the waves were topping a good 2 metres, the crests weren't breaking. This meant that as we turned east to pick our way round the next peninsula paddling in the regular rise and fall of the waves was enjoyable. All around us were dozens of rocky skerries upon which the waves exploded up and over providing excitement and drama for our first paddling for the day.

As we approached the headland of Rubha Bhruairnis a flight of fulmars appeared along the wave troughs, flashing past us without a single beat of their wings, then circling once to double-check us before skimming away seemingly millimetres above the wave crests. Once round the headland we negotiated our route carefully through a series of islets before surfing north into the next chain of island off-liers where the sea dropped a little and allowed us to raft up and catch our breaths for five minutes. To our north west lay the top end of Barra and the beach airfield of Tràigh Mhòr. Through the gaps in the islands around us we could occasionally make out the next stretch of our route via the islands of Hellisay and Gighay, the last land before leaving Barra and crossing to Eriskay.

We chose to hug the sheltered sides of all the islands and rocky outcrops on our way to Hellisay to make our journey less tiring and save some energy for the crossing to Eriskay over the Sound of Barra. This crossing, although not far, is exposed. During the Clearances over one hundred crofters from neighbouring islands and the mainland ended up on Hellisay. I was keen to stop off to potter round as it seemed incredible that so many people could survive on such a small rocky, thin-soiled island, less than 2 square kilometres in area; it was hard to imagine how they eked out a living on such a barren lump.

We pulled into the narrow gap between Hellisay and its immediate neighbour, Gighay, and 'anchored' our boats on a small area of kelp that broke the sea's surface. The wind was still freshening; even here in the shelter of the two islands the gusts funnelled through wrenching at our paddles as we sat discussing whether we should go ashore or push on. As I was concerned about the short crossing to the south tip of Eriskay we decided to press north and give it a go. We could always turn back and camp on Hellisay if the seas were too big on the crossing.

A few minutes later from the northwest side of Gighay we could see the white-capped sea running from right to left in front of us. The sky was by now very grey and low clouds seemed to suck all the light out of the day. A few kilometres to the west of us we could just make out the shape of the Eriskay-to-Barra ferry crashing square-bowed into the oncoming sea. The spray rose with each impact and flew up and over the vessel before the high bow ramp rose up again momentarily before the next plunge. We sat watching for a few minutes, eating a chocolate bar and deciding whether to go for it or turn back. With a quartering sea on our starboard stern we thought that it would be a brisk crossing. We paddled forward from our haven behind the rocky cliff and entered the melée before us. Fortunately, even though the waves were pretty big, they were at least going in roughly the direction we wanted: the sheltered west side of Eriskay. Following the initial push off into the waves we hardly put in a single forward stroke as the boats were picked up by wave after wave surging us forward with surprising speed. We couldn't now change our minds and retreat even if we wanted to. Fully loaded with food and camping gear, my flat-bowed kayak was heavy and low in the water. As I slid down the face of each wave the bow struggled to surface again. This was due to the bow digging deep into the trough and vanishing for a second or two as the water poured back as far as the forward hatch cover. I could see, off to my side, that Andrea's boat had a high bow that never once dipped under the surface. I vowed there and then that I'd had enough of this and would get a kayak the same as hers.

Our progress was rapid and in a very short time we drew level with the fragmented rocky outcrops to the south of Eriskay where every few seconds the waves made some spectacular explosions up the cliff faces. We stayed as far off land as we could, without going too far off course, to avoid the worst of the clapotis bouncing back off the cliffs. The journey along the west side of Eriskay became easier as the force of the sea died away the further we surfed, and by the time we pulled into the beach north of the new ferry slip, the water was glassy smooth. Tired from this crossing, we decided to camp on the grass above the beach. Our bows had hardly touched shore when a big brown and white collie appeared from the dunes above and dashed down to where we sat. In true mad-collie style it appeared to want us to play a game of throw and retrieve, except that every time we picked up a handy bit of drift wood or a kelp stipe and chucked it along the beach, the dog just stood and watched it. It took us a while to realise that it wasn't interested in long stick-like things but in smooth round stones. We wondered if perhaps there were no trees on the island and if it didn't know that sticks were perfect for chasing. In typical collie fashion, once we threw stones it badgered us continually for more.

Camp was set up as we watched the ferry return from Barra. That was its last journey of the afternoon as sea and weather condtions had deteriorated. The three cars in the queue presumably turned round to try again the next day. Our camping spot was a good one, thick, well-drained grass on top of the dunes. Had the weather been fine we would have had an amazing view to the west. We were too tired to wander over to the Politician pub for a pint so called it a day fairly early in the evening. The wind howled high over our camp and through the night the rain battered the tent several times. I woke at some point and went out to check the tent and boats. In the dark, I dashed quickly out of the tent door, wearing nothing but a pair of wellies to keep the sheep pooh off my feet. As I sallied forth into the wet, windy (and rather chilly) darkness I stumbled over a dark shape at my feet and plunged flat out onto the grass (and the ubiquitous sheep droppings). Our friend the collie had been sleeping by the front opening of the tent. Thinking that I wanted to play again, it bounded up and presented its stone next to my shivering body. After tightening the guy ropes and trying to shoo the mutt away I was glad to get back to the warmth of the sleeping bag and stayed put through the rest of the night.

In the early hours of the morning the low pressure system moved on, unlike the collie, which was still there and no amount of cajoling could make it leave. My last memory of Eriskay, as we set off that morning was the dog standing in the water by the shore, expectantly waiting for that last stone throw. It finally give up, turned and bounded off back inland, no doubt to find some new unsuspecting person to attach itself to.

At the top end of the island where the new causeway joined Eriskay to South Uist only a narrow channel was left open to allow water flow between the two sides. We had the option of passing through it to paddle up the east side of the Uists or to try our luck on the more exposed west side. If we were on the west side in bad weather coming in from the Atlantic we could find ourselves stranded. The virtually straight coast which ran for over 30 kilometres due north was an amazing series of endless big sandy beaches. In Scotland, it seems that if a few days of low pressure systems pass over, it will be replaced with a high pressure that typically lasts for a couple of days. As the morning was bright, with sun, no wind, and flat seas we elected to go for the west side which promised to be benign for once. Even so, the ever-present Atlantic swell produced some impressive dumping-seas onto the beaches to our right as we began the long paddle north.

The paddling was easy and we were in no particular rush. We were on our second last day before joining up with Graham and family. We were also still tired from the previous day's exertions and for some time we relaxed and enjoyed the steadily rising temperature of the day. The flat coastal land of South Uist varied little as we progressed although we could see the hills on the far side rising spectacularly behind. We occasionally saw a person or two walking on the magnificent beaches as we passed them one after the other. Our only landing that morning was at a little sheltered point where the surf was low enough to go easily ashore for a coffee and a break. At this point on the coast, Rubha Aird a' Mhuile, the map indicated a 'Danger Area' with multiple labels in bright red font. The top half of the island on this side was a MOD missile testing range and we weren't quite sure what to do to get past. As the weather seemed settled we thought it best to stop early for the day and set up camp. There was a track running near to us which meant we could abandon the trip here if necessary. Nevertheless, I was keen to get to the top end of the island if at all possible.

The afternoon was spent in well-earned bliss snoozing in the sun and pottering around. The next day we awoke to equally bright conditions although through the night the wind had got up a little. We decided to push on north and see what happened. Our one concession to the danger of the rocket range was to paddle a few kilometres or so offshore so that we could sneak past the main part of the range and slip unnoticed onto the next island of Benbecula – or so we thought. All went well for the first few hours. Occasionally overhead we could hear something flying past heading in the direction of St Kilda. After a while this stopped and a short time later a small plane, the size of a radio-controlled model, buzzed over before landing under a large white floppy parachute.

By this time we were quite far out from the shore and were pleased with our progress. The sea had set into an easy 2-foot chop, which we assumed would provide the perfect cover for our passage north. As we drew level with a place on the map annotated with 'DANGER AREA' in upper case letters, we could see a large fast RIB boat scudding southwards a good kilometre inshore from us. We were beginning to suspect that something was afoot. Our suspicions grew as it turned offshore and made directly for us. Woops! We were sprung.

The guys on this range safety boat were very good humoured. We were their first call out for a week or so, their last target having been a wind surfer whom they couldn't catch. All they could do was chase him off the range. They said that they could escort us, or we could simply haul our kayaks onto the inflatable sponsons of their boat and they would give us a lift north. Being lazy, we chose the latter. Apparently we had been spotted from a long way off but the range manager had decided to continue testing Rapier missiles until we were right under the flight path. We learned that the small plane was a radio-controlled target drone that flew a figure of eight course just a few kilometres off St Kilda. The Rapier missiles were then launched at this plane to test them. What was a bit worrying was that they hardly ever hit it – even though its exact whereabouts was known. Needless to say, we were more than a little embarrassed about the whole event but we saved a few kilometres of paddling and enjoyed the lift in the RIB. The banter was good and it turned out that these guys were from Skye, where, of course we had a bunch of mutual friends.

The last 10 kilometres north up the west side of Benbecula were comparatively uneventful. We reached Balivanich where we would finish our trip. Later that day Graham came to collect us and take us to Lochmaddy where he and his family were staying. When we went into the hotel bar that evening the first person we bumped into was Andrea's boss who was doing some veterinary work in the area. His first words were, 'Ah, so it was you two that got hauled off the rocket range after all. I thought it would be…' There is no better grapevine than on the Uists.

Best meal on trip: kedgeree (serves 2-3)

2 hard boiled eggs, chopped into large pieces
¾ of a mug of rice
1 onion, chopped
1 tsp curry powder
1 small carton of single cream
2 small smoked haddock (vacuum packed)
Add water (twice the volume of rice) and cook. Cover the pan and bring to

a simmer for 5 minutes. Put to one side. Fry the onions in butter until soft. Add the curry powder. Put the rice back on the burner if required. Add all the ingredients together and heat through before serving. Serve with fresh bread and butter and a good dry white wine.

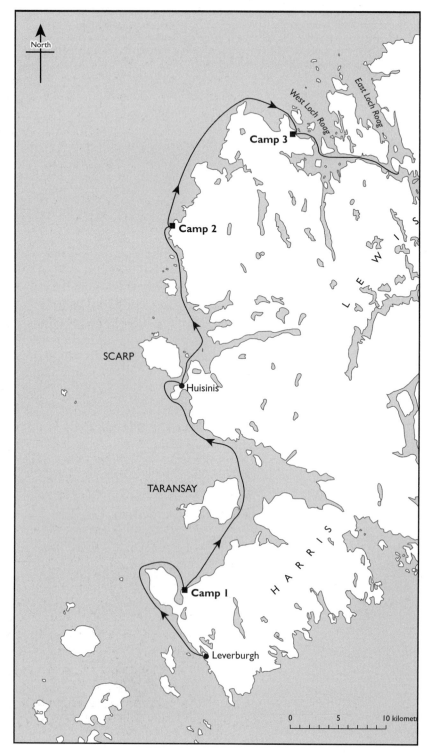

Above: Andrea at south end of Arran with Ailsa Craig on the horizon
Below: Baldy Clady's Bothy, Islay

Above: Andrea entering Loch Roag
Below: Campsite at Loch Roag

Above: Stopping for water at Loch Roag
Below: Waiting to launch at the Sound of Harris

Above: Campsite at Erraid, Mull
Below: Flat sea, south of Oban

Above: Mark leading the way on the Crinan Canal
Below: The author sliding into the Crinan Canal

Above: The top locks of the Crinan Canal
Below: The puffer, *Vital Spark*, on the Crinan Canal

Above: Mark passing under low bridge on the Crinan Canal
Below: Graham and the author off Pabbay

Above: Campsite on Vatersay with the 'doubles' site visible in the background
Below: Beginning the crossing between Sandray and Pabbay

Above: Andrea coming ashore on Mingulay
Below: Graham relaxing with roll-up after bumpy crossing to Pabbay

Above left: Clan chief's headstone at ruined chapel, Inch Kenneth. Above right: Flotsam and dream-catcher, Skipness Beach
Below left: Worn cross at ruined chapel, Colonsay. Below right: Font at ruined chapel Colonsay

Above left: Mark preparing the pears in mead, Loch Fyne. Above right: Joe's 50th birthday celebration, Inch Kenneth
Below left: Graham developing cabin fever, Vatersay. Below right: Rusty steam boiler by the abandoned basking shark factory, Soay

Above: Landing on the west coast of Harris
Below: Lifting fog, Harris

Above: Campsite on Eigg. An Sgurr in the background
Below: New pier on Eigg. Dug-out canoe in foreground

Above: Filling water containers at the Bridge over the Atlantic, Seil
Below: Hitching a lift from Mallaig to Rum on a tug

Above: Mark approaching Inveraray
Below: The author coming ashore at Inveraray

Above left: Skirting the north of Skye. Above right: Andrea coming ashore in perfect conditions, North Uist
Below left: The journey's end, Loch Roag. Below right: An unsure Mark about to be dropped into the
Crinan Canal

Chapter 5

Leverburgh to Callanish in fog

Our voyage to Mingulay, Barra and the Uists had been so rewarding that we returned many times for short spells to the central part of the Western Isles. Lapping up the tranquility and remoteness of long golden sands around the top end of North Uist and Berneray was eminently satisfying. On one such visit, Andrea having spent several days sexing farmed salmon for future brood stock (someone has to do it!), we camped on the north-east coast of Berneray and relaxed in late summer warmth, paddling along the coast and wandering on the quiet strands.

On the second day we paddled to the small islands of Pabbay and Shillay, to the north of Berneray. The sun was strong in the sky and the sea flat calm. The paddle over to Pabbay was straightforward and we relished the settled conditions. We knew that autumnal gales would soon begin their long months of battering the land, shaping and re-shaping the beaches, throwing kelp and other sea débris far inshore. Pabbay had once been almost joined to Berneray by such a fine stretch of sand that legend has it that a woman could throw her washing from one side of the narrow channel to the other. Sadly, it is not recorded why she would wish to do this. We stopped briefly on Pabbay for a walk past numerous dead hulks of rusty landrovers, abandoned forever where they finally broke down when they couldn't be patched up one more time. Dumping vehicles on crofts is a peculiar feature of the Western Isles. Occasionally they are temporarily re-employed as chicken coops or dog kennels. Rusty vehicles of many generations clogging up farmyards blight the landscape but it has been difficult to dispose of them until recently.

Before the infamous Highland Clearances Pabbay was a well-farmed island and home to 300 people. One of the benefits of the rich barley harvest was a fine production of illicit whisky, and in such a remote place that would be cut off for weeks at a time in the winter storms, a good slug of the 'water of life' would be a welcome restorative during the damp, dark evenings. The only slight problem with this was that no taxes were paid to the government and there was the ever present danger of excise men making a surprise visit. There are no longer active distilleries on the Western Isles, or at least any that are known to the authorities.

Keen to push on to Shillay, we paddled round the west side of Pabbay and crossed the final narrow Sound of Shillay to pass between the outlying island of Little Shillay and Shillay itself. Little Shillay was a craggy lump and the sea in the short passage between the two islands was quite rough but as we circled the island the water quickly calmed down. A few kilometres to our north-east, on the other side of the Sound of Harris, the hill of Ceapabhal at the oddly named Toe Head on Harris, stood high over the surrounding land. The paddle across would have been short but being time-limited we carried on round Shillay.

The coast of Shillay was rather grand, with cliffs and clefts all round the north side. These were lower on the south side where we pulled into the short stretch of smooth sandy beach. It was just past midday and the sun was beating down on us as we prepared lunch. We had been passing grey seals all day and here at Shillay a large number played just off the beach; some of the males were gigantic and made their presence known by the occasional leap out of the sea, crashing back down with a thump and big splash of water.

For once, it was so hot that we braved the waters for a cooling swim before heading back to Berneray. Much later, I learned that in 1946 a local fisherman landed a lobster from Shillay that was 35 inches long, 15 inches in circumference, with 7.5 inches of cutting edge on the scissors claw and the empty shell weighed almost 11 pounds. Best not to know what's down there! There could have been a different take on the *Jaws* story – *Claws*! At least when we had grappled the creature to its death, we could have it for lunch.

A previous trip to this area had, however, turned out rather differently. Following a week of wonderful weather, and with a fairly promising forecast, we had caught the Uig to Tarbert ferry and travelled down to An t'Ob to begin a trip up the west side of Harris and Lewis to Loch Roag. An t'Ob is also known as Leverburgh, the Island of Harris and Lewis having been bought in 1918 by the soap magnate, Lord Leverhulme. He tried to do his best for the population, from gifting crofts to developing the fishing fleet. Unfortunately, when he passed away in 1925 his dream died with him. Poverty followed and over 1,000 men emigrated to North America. Although the small village was renamed after him it is still widely known as An t'Ob.

We arrived at An t'Ob before lunch, popped into the café for coffee and baked potato before packing the boats in the damp fine rain and trolleying them down to the ferry slip. We stood to one side for a while whilst the Berneray to Harris ferry came in. This had been the first time I'd been here since the events of a snowy Sunday morning in April earlier that year when just before 10 o'clock in the morning a little piece of Hebridean history was made. On that occasion the ferry, *MV Loch Portain,* eased its way up to the slipway, lowered its ramp, and a few cars and slightly more foot passengers arrived on the first Sunday sailing to Harris. The restriction on Sunday sailings had now ended and perhaps a little of the power of the Free Presbyterian church was lost. Unfortunately, the timing was insensitive as the Free Presbyterian church that overlooks Leverburgh harbour was celebrating one of its six-monthly communion services.

One of the deck crew proffered some good advice on the route through the Sound of Harris, qualified by, 'Don't do it in anything smaller than a decent-sized ship if the sea is running against the tide.' The Sound is a shallow channel and the Atlantic swell often runs slap bang into the west-going tide making for some really dire conditions. At least today the conditions were fairly benign: grey skies, drizzle, light winds, and the occasional late season midge having a bite. We waited until the ferry pulled out, then, with a last wave to the deckhand, we slid into the sound and turned North West.

Within a minute or two of leaving the slip we met with a group of otters, a mother and three cubs, swimming on the surface and coming from the other side of the sound. They were working hard in the stiff current and with hardly a turn of their heads they powered past us and, seconds later, landed on the rocks behind us. With a momentary shake of their coats to shed the water they quickly climbed up on to the grass above and vanished behind a small rise on the banking. It was good to see them especially since we didn't see another otter on the whole trip.

The ebb tide running south-east was not too strong against us through the sound and we made good time to the beach at Tràigh na Cleabhaig and the narrow part of the peninsula we were about to circuit. From here it was only a 500 metre portage to the north side of the isthmus and although we contemplated nipping over using our trolleys to carry the kayaks, it seemed like cheating. Instead we carried on to Toe Head, the oddly named headland at the top end of the sound. Shillay was just 6 or 7 kilometres away but it wasn't visible in the murk. The sea was bigger than when we had left the shelter of the sound and by the time we reached the headland at Gob an Tobha (another Ob name derivative) there were 3–4 foot waves coming in from the North West. Our original plan had been to head due north to camp on the island of Taransay but battling the sea head-on would have been hard work. We turned round the headland and made for the big beach at Scarasta.

With the growing swell on our port beam we had a few good lifts forward and the waves were the perfect size for surfing down even though the boats were heavy with food and camping gear. I hadn't realised just how lacking in energy Andrea was until she called for a tow for the last couple of kilometres. This was fairly straightforward initially but as the waves grew in the shallowing waters they began to rise up quite steeply and break over us heavily. The tow rope was a good 12 metres in length with built-in bungy cords to absorb any snatching. When, however, we were on different parts of waves, Andrea in the trough of one and me on the forward face of another, the jolting motion suddenly held back the boat on a downwards surf, which had the effect of dragging the stern under the water of the following wave, sending the bow skywards and making the boat very unstable for a few seconds. We bolted and jolted forward for a good half an hour or so until the landing came into view. We un-hitched the tow rope to make our final run into the dumping surf.

The main Scarasta beach was too hazardous to land on because of our heavy boats which could easily be damaged. Furthermore, there were too many houses above the beach for us to find a good spot to camp. Just to the north of the main beach was a small headland with a few offshore reefs and a small sandy patch that looked suitable. After dodging some spectacular breaks over the reefs we snaked inside the chaos and tried to work out the timing of the surf on the shore. In the end we gave up as there seemed to be no obvious pattern. I shot in first and did pretty well, landing on a pile of storm-washed kelp, lying two-feet deep on the sand. As I scrambled out of the boat I was caught and soaked by the next wave. Andrea considered her approach carefully and made it all look so easy running in on the back of a breaker and landing so delicately on the seaweed next to my dripping self.

We set up camp, changed and then sat in the porch of the tent on our rather nice new thermarest chairs drinking coffee and eating chocolate, watching the surf crashing on the beach below us. Even though Scarista House restaurant, whose cuisine was reputed for its use of good local produce was nearby, we opted for our own mundane pasta and tomato sauce.

By morning the sea had calmed right down and settled into a rather eerie stillness. We were quickly off and crossed over to the island of Taransay, the location for the well-known television programme 'Castaway 2000'. We skirted the east side of the island. Neither of us wished to go ashore as we were keen to press on while conditions were good. Ahead, past the north coast of the island lay the shores of Harris but in the thick bank of sea fog that was developing we could see nothing but grey. We set our compasses on the promontory of A' Chailleach (the witch) a few kilometres away and paddled into the enveloping fog. The going was hard and staying in sight of each other in the thick grey murk was not easy. Visibility quickly dropped to 5 metres and the cold of the fine water droplets that covered everything became heat-sapping. Fortunately, the sea was calm. A couple of times during the crossing we lost sight of each other for a few moments. Making out where Andrea's shouts were coming from in the mist was very difficult and we were relieved to meet up again, more by luck than anything else.

Trapped in the fog on the relatively calm sea it was the sound of the breaking swell that made us realise that we were almost at the rocks on the other side. We turned westwards and kept the sound of the surf on our right-hand side. Our first stop was in the narrow inlet of Loch Gobhaig where it was good to see land again and pull ashore for a bite to eat. Had the ground here been flat and not so boggy we would happily have stopped for the day as concentrating so hard in the fog, partly to keep sight of each other and partly to maintain a safe distance off the rocks, was very tiring. More tiring was the tension of keeping an accurate compass bearing to avoid accidentally paddling out to sea. The risk of being mown down by another vessel kept our own noise to a minimum and our ears sharpened to any strange sounds that might herald the approach of a boat.

We carried on and soon turned north. To our left lay a series of reefs, over which we could hear the swell breaking. As we would not see a breaking sea 10 feet in front of us in this thick mist we stayed close to the main shore and its own set of breaking waves. Somehow, this seemed safer as the shore offered potential safety, although whether or not we could clamber up the rocks if the worst came to the worst was another matter. To our north lay another small peninsula at Huisinis around which we had to pass to reach the safety of the Sound of Scarp. When we passed the offshore reefs on our port beam we, perhaps rather rashly, took a new bearing for the headland one kilometre away and struck across the bay to meet it. Fifteen minutes later, by sheer fluke, we slid right under the cliff at the point and then turned north-east into the sound, pulling up on the foreshore by the jetty and a well-earned stop for lunch.

The grassy parkland above us marked the end of the small winding road that starts on the shores of West Loch Tarbert just by the ruins of the whaling station at Bun Abhainn Eadarra which had been built before the

First World War by Norwegians and abandoned in the 1930s. The road picks its way along the shore of the loch, past the castle of Amhuinnsuidhe. The castle was built in 1868 by the Earl of Dunsmore next to some spectacular slabbed waterfalls and a river noted for its ample salmon runs. It was here that the author James Barrie of *Peter Pan* fame, wrote his lesser known drama, *Mary Rose*, inspired by the dramatic scenery of the surrounding lochs and hills.

Our own, slightly less inspired, comfort came from a wonderful lunch of Heinz tomato soup and home-made fruit cake, not quite *haute cuisine* but perfect in our eyes. In front of us the fog lifted a little and from the top of the jetty we could just see the rocky coast of Scarp across the other side of the sound. As with many rocky Scottish islands, life was difficult here for the inhabitants of old. Eeking a living out of the ground was extremely hard work. It was, however, not the hunger and privations of the people of Scarp that gives it a place in world history but the events that followed the hardship of Mrs Christina MacLennan in 1934. Having given birth to a healthy child on the 14th January, the following day she felt poorly. As there was no means of communication on the island an islander rowed across the sound to phone for help from Huisinis but found the phone out of order. Consequently, the local postman's son was dispatched by bus to Tarbert to fetch the doctor from there. When the doctor finally arrived on Scarp he decided that Christina should go to hospital in Stornoway. The journey, first by open boat over the bumpy Sound of Scarp, then by bus to hospital, must have been a nightmare for her, but her misery turned to joy when the cause of her suffering turned out to be a second child that was duly born – on the 15th. As the twins were born on different dates, on different islands and in different counties, the national press took note.

But the story doesn't end there. The event came to the ears of a young German scientist, Gerhard Zucher, who came to Scarp to try out novel technology for transporting mail between islands using a one-metre-long solid-fuel rocket that could fly at 1,000 mph. After several test launches, the day came for him to pack his rocket with hundreds of pieces of mail. Unfortunately, his rocket exploded on the launch pad and the mail was scattered far and wide across Scarp. The island's postmaster retrieved a large number of scorched letters and dispatched them by boat. To explain the burnt edges of the letters he stamped them with the words 'Damaged by first explosion at Scarp – Harris'. Following a second trial the experiment to link the island to Harris was abandoned. Herr Zucher was later to attain greater notoriety for his role in the development of the World War Two German V2 rocket programme. His name, however, lived on in the Western Isles and in recent times a film, *Rocket Post,* about the events on the island was filmed on Taransay and subsequently screened throughout Scotland.

We took to the water again and set off to the most remote part of west Harris. From here, northwards, there were no access roads leading to the sea for another 12 kilometres or so. Within ten minutes of paddling we slid past the golden beach of Tràigh Mheilein, the water sparkling green-blue over the bright sand below our boats. Compared to the otherwise monochromatic surroundings earlier in the day this was a real jewel.

As we left the beach behind us, we could see three sea lochs carving into the rugged Harris hills and it was tempting to make a series of detours to explore them. We decided to resist the temptation and push on to the north and set up camp near the slipway that was marked on the map opposite the island of Mealasta. This also heralded the beginning of the roads again, and the possibility of escape if the weather turned nasty. It was a long slog across the mouths of the lochs, running from headland to headland in an attempt to make the crossing of Bràigh Mòr easier in a series of smaller steps. By three in the afternoon we slipped between the mainland and Eilean Mhealasta. We realised later that we were now at the coast of Lewis. The islands of Harris and Lewis are one landmass but identified as two islands. At some point we had crossed the 'border'.

As the slip at Mealasta was not very inviting we found a little beach a short distance to the north. We set up camp in a small enclosed grassy field with a wall all around which would provide shelter and a handy place to air our damp, slightly smelly kayaking clothes. Above our camp were the remains of an army camp. The bleak concrete buildings were stubbornly resisting the continual blast of the winter storms and provided welcome shelter for generations of sheep. The huts were built on the site of an old Benedictine convent and somewhere near to here were traces of an underground chamber.

Lewis is well known for its underground treasures. In 1831, the remains of at least four complete chess sets were found hidden in a sand-dune at Uig. The Norse chessmen, which were made of walrus or whale-tooth ivory, date from the 12th century. There are several different and colourful theories about how the hoard came to be. Were they stolen from a passing ship or hidden by a travelling salesman? The pieces were first displayed at the Society of Antiquaries in Scotland in 1831. Eleven pieces are currently owned by the National Museums of Scotland and the remaining eighty-two are in the British Museum. While the reason for the hoard is unknown, there is little doubt that chess would have been a pastime of the wealthy Viking lords who ruled the islands at the time, paying lip service to the King in Norway, but fighting endlessly amongst themselves for local control. The chessmen depict contemporary Norse characters and the excellent craftsmanship is contrary to the usual stereotype Viking raider. While the first Viking invasion of the Hebrides was in the 9th century, the islands continued to be colonised by Norwegians until the time of King Haakon of Norway who was defeated by King Alexander III at the Battle of Largs in 1263. The Western Isles then passed to a Scottish king in 1266 under the Treaty of Perth.

A few years ago there was an amusing incident relating to the Lewis chessmen. A dead sperm whale that had been washed up on the west coast of Lewis had been transported to the Stornoway tip. The official plan was to extract the whale's teeth when the carcass had rotted in order to create a replica of the Lewis chessmen. A couple of locals, however, had a similar plan and one night they broke into the tip and proceeded to steal the teeth from the whale. The CCTV cameras caught their images but although the enterprising thieves had been prepared for this and had worn balaclavas, they were identified: their collie dog was recognised by the police and gave the game away.

The old metal military-built road over the rise behind us looked as though no one had maintained it for many a decade. Nevertheless, this did not deter a surprising number of cars and camper vans throughout the afternoon and evening. The camper vans stayed put for the night. As I get older, much to my horror, my mind turns more and more to the thought of buying one of these mobile homes. It would be marvellous not to set up a soggy tent at the end of a day of outdoor activity and cook crouched in a tiny nylon porch desperately trying to avoid the midges and rain. A similarly-minded friend recently bought a camper van magazine and we were amazed by a whole new world of equipment and clever design. We were even more amazed by the cost: £20,000 would get you going with a pretty basic model, whereas something more luxurious would make your bank manager wince.

The weather remained settled that evening. Sitting on the grass by the tent, we calculated that there were 18 kilometres to Gallan Head. The coast to this point could be exposed to high seas from the west and there would be no islands or channels to provide protection. If the weather would hold for one more day we would have the trip 'in the can'.

Early next morning I poked my head out of the tent to take stock. The fog had returned with a vengeance. I could just make out the edge of the water below us. It seemed calm and there was no sound of waves breaking on the rocks at the sides of the little bay. Whilst not relishing the prospect of another day of compass following in zero visibility, I reckoned that the flat sea would make for an easy passage north. We broke camp and pushed off into the cold, grey dampness.

For the next 7 kilometres it was like being in a sensory deprivation tank, travelling within a cocoon of dampness with all visual clues removed: grey sea, grey walls and a grey ceiling. When paddling side by side we could tell which way was up, but when further apart, on the edge of the visibility fuzzy-bubble, it was very difficult to maintain balance and several times I almost capsized before catching myself with a last-second bracing stroke. Eventually I adopted a technique for making a large splash with my leading paddle blade as it dug into the water which ruffled the surface of the sea enough to allow me to work out what was sea and what was fog.

This reminded me of a solo trip I had made from Applecross to Plockton, crossing the wide mouth of Loch Kishorn to make landfall by Plockton airfield. The weather was hot and humid, and the sea was glassy smooth, the surrounding hills mirrored on its surface. I felt I was paddling in some other-worldly state – neither water nor air. Even though I could see the land in the distance, when I looked down at the area in front of my kayak I was unable to judge which way was up or which way was down. It was a strange sensation, almost as though, at any point you were going to fall off the water surface and down into another deeper place. On that occasion also I resorted to making over-exaggerated splashes with my paddle blade to highlight the surface of the water.

Navigation in the thick fog was proving almost impossible. The best we could do was to take a bearing from the map, stick rigidly to it, and then by timing ourselves, expect to reach a planned landmark such as a major indentation in the coast or a change in coastal direction. We would turn sharp right to aim for a designated point and then attempt to clarify our position when the edge of the coast appeared out of the gloom. This didn't work too well and we took an age to travel up to the township of Mangurstadh which we identified purely from the sound of car engines and the change in course of the coast line from north-east to north-west.

By late morning, high above us we could occasionally see cliffs emerging from the grey as bit by bit the fog showed signs of lifting. Gaining in confidence, we took a bearing to take us through the gap between the mainland and the little rocky island of Eilean Molach. This route would take us further offshore. Suddenly we heard an almighty crash and splash only a few metres behind us. We spun round to see an area of froth and the circle of wavelets running out from a central point. For all our years of paddling and seeing and hearing grey seals, basking sharks and porpoises, we had never experienced such a sudden explosion of water and loud noise. As we paddled like fury away from the area we wondered what it might have been. Whatever it was, we didn't want to be near it a second time. Just as we regained control of our racing heartbeats and were settling down again, a fast fishing launch shot out of the mist and flew past our bows, only 15 metres away, vanishing back into the gloom just as fast as he had appeared. The sound of the engine was so muffled by the fog that it was lost to us within seconds.

This really scared us and made us realise just how vulnerable we were in this mist. We had not heard it approach until it was right on us. We had thought that we would hear vessels approaching and that in any case a right-minded skipper would be travelling very slowly in low visibility. How wrong we were on both accounts. We turned east a little to make for the safety of the cliffs as quickly as we could. Thankfully, the mist was now breaking into patches and the first of the sunshine was making itself felt. Until this moment I hadn't realised how cold I was and it was sheer luxury to lean back in the cockpit and soak up the warmth.

As we approached the narrow gap between Eilean Molach and the rocky main coast we just managed to make our way through. What a spectacle! Sheer cliffs rose from the water's edge. The rocks were stunning in deep reds, with a definite metallic hue to the smooth wet surface. As we drew level with the island a great chasm opened up and we could see a tunnel running right through the island. It was an amazing sight and one for which we had to stop to photograph. We could now relax to enjoy the scenery after the trauma of the last few kilometres – the mysterious sea creature and the mad fisherman. In contrast to the dullness of the fog, the colours of the rocks appeared heightened as we sat bobbing in the narrow channel. We considered trying to squeeze through the cleft but we reckoned that we wouldn't be lucky a third time and decided to press on. Round the next small headland we turned into a small sandy bay and stopped for lunch. With the demise of the fog, the wind was now picking up. To our north we could see the coast running up towards Gallan Head and the entrance to Loch Roag. It was becoming a bit bouncy out to sea and the first few white caps were breaking.

Most big headlands give rise to a slight feeling of trepidation. These are places that attract currents and big seas and inevitably they are also significant milestones on routes as they usually herald a completion of a section of coast or the end of the trip. The tide was on the rise as we approached. The sea was bumpy but it was preferable to being back in the gloom of the mist. When the high-cliffed headland appeared we were in good paddling form and ready for a bouncy passage round. Fortunately, this didn't happen and we slipped past very close in, enjoying the clapotis of the waves bouncing off the base of the wall. Metres later we tucked ourselves in behind the shelter of the point and relaxed again for the second time that day, pleased to be in the wide open mouth of Loch Roag. Another successful trip. From here we could spend a day or two pottering around the loch.

Stretched out in front of us, as far as the eye could see, lay the enormous expanse of the loch. The main body measures some 12 kilometres square with several further smaller offshoots extending deep into the Lewis heartland. Within the loch are numerous islands and reefs, ranging from Great Bernera, some 7 kilometres long, which splits the main loch into two, down to hundreds of sharp rocky reefs dotted around making for tricky navigation in anything but a small craft.

Surrounding the loch are countless small freshwater lochans and streams that are excellent for salmon and trout fishing. Grimersta, designated by the European Union as a Special Area of Conservation for Atlantic Salmon, has caused controversy over the years because of so many salmon farms in the loch. The wild fish lobby argues that sea lice from the caged fish transfer to the migrating adult salmon and smolts, aggravating the decline of the species on Scotland's west coast. Whilst there might be some truth in this it is not the whole story. Fishermen are all too ready to point a finger of blame. Saw-billed ducks, herons, seals, and otters have all been accused at sometime or other of decimating fish stocks but most predators have co-existed with salmon from time immemorial. Man, including fishermen, are most likely the main culprits in upsetting the natural balance. For many decades, well-intentioned riparian owners chucked eggs and fry indiscriminately into local rivers. This is now recognised as an almost futile means of enhancing stocks.

The early afternoon sun to the south of us was a real tonic. We stripped off our heavy cagoules and paddled across the first set of inlets in our T-shirts towards Caolas Pabaigh official campsite past the oddly named village of Cnip. Coming into the sound, the rocks on our right were indented with some spectacularly long and narrow caves. We entered a couple but the sudden drop in temperature inside soon drove us back out. As we needed some water we landed and ambled up to houses at the next inlet where a woman was dashing round her vegetable plot constantly bending down picking things up and throwing them over the fence. It transpired that her garden was overrun with large snails, which were actively consuming her lettuces and potatoes. She hated them but couldn't bring herself to kill them, hence the aerial redistribution on a regular basis. We filled our water sacks at her outside tap and left her to her molluscan campaign. Ten minutes later we arrived at the beach and set up our tent in a secluded spot in the dunes near to one side of the main grassy area. That evening we lay on the short sheep-sheared machair drinking a nice full-bodied white wine and watching the sun set over the entrance to the loch.

The next day we wandered over to a small loch behind the campsite. It was teeming with trout. The highlight of the day, apart from the desperately needed lie-in was to luxuriate (albeit with a touch of comedy) in the shower for as long as the £1 coin lasted. So as not to waste one second of my five-minute shower I set my clean dry clothes, soap and towel neatly in the first of the two cubicles, stripped off, thrust my £1 into the slot and dived back into the cubicle, soap in hand. Nothing happened. A second of two later I heard the whoosh of streaming hot water – in the next door cubicle!

The sun shone strongly for the entire day and we lapped up every second of it. The Trangia was put on again and again to produce endless cups of coffee which we drank with ginger nuts and chocolate: indulgent but heavenly. The afternoon was spent drying every bit of kit out and making sure all was well with our boats. We found an old copy of *The Herald* in the back hold of one and finished the crossword. It was a pity that we were two years too late to try for the prize. Could we claim poor postal services from Lewis?

The next morning we were up and away early to finish the short paddle into the head of the loch and ultimately to Callanish where our journey would end. We picked our way past the islands of Fuigh Mòr and Fuigh Beag. From there we entered the narrows that led to the narrow channel that separated Great Bernera from Lewis. We paddled under the low pre-stressed concrete bridge (the first of its type to be built in Europe) that links the two islands. The bridge was constructed when the locals threatened to construct a causeway across the channel by blasting away at the nearby hill. The currents run strongly through the channel and years back, after a few days of tedious work in the area, I remember jumping off the bridge into the fast flowing channel with a couple of colleagues to celebrate the end of our sojourn there. We were wearing baggy dry suits and by the time we flopped and flapped to shore we had been carried a good few hundred metres down the channel. We had clearly omitted a 'risk assessment' and we realised that our Health and Safety officer would have had 'meltdown' had he known.

From here we pottered the last few kilometres to the jetty below the standing stones at Callanish. Megalithic structures, typically circles and avenues, are evocative places and the stones at Callanish are among the most haunting. Not only is there the imposing physical presence of the stones in a spectacular landscape, there is also an atmosphere of mystery. The stones tower to a height of nearly four metres and the main monument covers an area of some 5,000 square metres. The circle itself is relatively modest and comprises thirteen upright stones with a huge megalith at the centre marking a later burial cairn. The main monument, built from local gneiss stone, dates back to around 3,000 BC when Lewis was populated by Stone Age farmers who lived in small villages dotted around the Outer Hebridean islands. The stability of the structures was clearly important and low mounds of earth and stones were added to the base of each upright structure because of the difficulty of digging sufficiently deep sockets. The central stone was set in place at this time and it is likely that the three rows running away to the south, east and west were added soon afterwards, together with an avenue which today comprises twenty stones and runs to the north. When the site was first excavated in 1857 a deep layer of peat had to be cleared away to reveal the true height of the stones, which, it is believed, were originally intended for ceremonies and ritual.

That was it, the trip was over. We retired to the Callanish visitor centre coffee shop for chips and pizza. Andrea drew the short straw and had to take a bus and then hitch back to An t'Ob for the car.

Best meal on trip: couscous, chick peas and vegetables

Small cup of couscous
Olive oil
1 onion, chopped
1 carrot, diced fairly small
1 small aubergine, cubed
1 can of chick peas
1 can of chopped tomatoes
2 spring onions, chopped
1 vegetable stock cube
2 tablespoons of chopped parsley
1 tablespoon of chopped coriander
1 cinnamon stick
2 cloves of garlic, chopped
1 teaspoon of coriander seed
1 teaspoon of cumin seed

Bring water (twice the volume of couscous) to the boil. Add the couscous. Put to one side for 6-8 minutes to cook. When cooked, add a little olive oil to separate the grains. For the sauce, heat the oil and fry the onions and spring onions until soft. Add the garlic, cumin, coriander, cinnamon stick and fry for a further minute or so. Add the fresh herbs, carrots, aubergines and chickpeas. Add the chopped tomatoes, stock cube and a little water. Simmer until the vegetables are cooked, but not pulped.

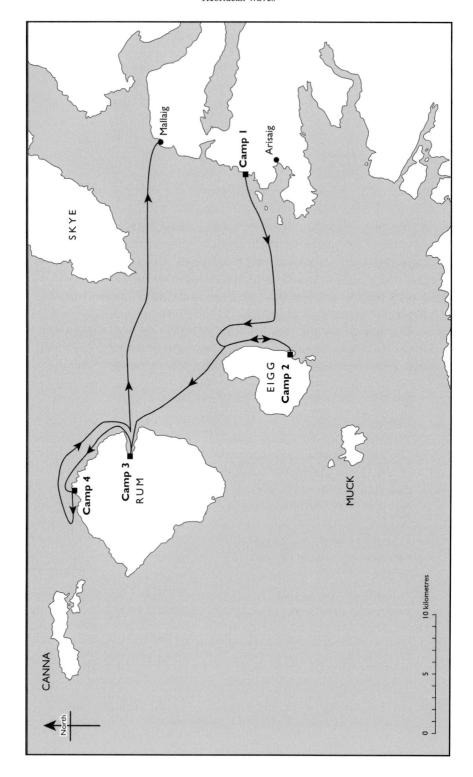

Chapter 6

Eigg, Rum, and almost Canna

The Inner Hebrides, a swathe of about thirty islands, lie east of the Outer Hebrides and south of Skye to the west of the Kintyre peninsula. The most northern of these, Eigg, Muck, Rum and Canna are known as The Small Isles. Each island has its own distinctive character and atmosphere. The low fertile lands of Muck, with attractive shell-sand beaches, contrast vividly with the long proud distinctive profile of Eigg and its cock-comb hill, An Sgurr. Rum, a brooding dark isle, once known as the 'forbidden island', sits in the background behind Eigg draped in heavy cloud for much of the year. Tucked out of sight behind Eigg and Rum, is Canna, the most westerly and the jewel in the crown of The Small Isles.

Previously owned by John Lorne Campbell, Canna was presented to the National Trust for Scotland in 1981. The island has ten working crofts and a population of sixteen. My first visit had been years earlier with the diving charter boat, *MV Kylebhan*, when we had to run for shelter during a storm. We lay alongside the pier until boredom set us jumping off the quayside in our dry suits but wearing our neoprene diving helmets back to front. Later on, in the dark of the stormy night, we dived for scallops under the boat assuming it would be a place commercial scallopers didn't bother with. Sometime later we emerged from under the hull with handfuls of scallops. The next day, after a hairy dive in the swell by an offshore reef we spent the afternoon wandering around the island. We were struck by the majesty of the place, from the idyllic Canna House surrounded by thick forest to the high sea cliffs behind.

Many years later I was looking forward to returning by kayak. For Andrea, James, Mark, Lesley and myself, Canna was to be the final destination in a trip from The Back of Keppoch on the mainland to Eigg, Rum and then Canna. After a night on the campsite at Keppoch we packed our boats and persuaded James that a few hundred chocolate bars were not the best diet for the coming trip; happily, we had enough food to go around. As we slipped the heavily laden boats into the water and struck out for the south end of Eigg, only 16 kilometres away, my mind was full of previous visits.

Some people have premonitions of sadness and disaster which in Scotland is called 'second sight'. My great auntie once related a childhood experience of walking down a narrow road near her house and stopping to let a funeral procession go by. She asked who it was for and was told it was for a local lad whom she knew. However, as far as she was aware this lad was still very much alive; she had seen him earlier that day. Confused, she ran back home but didn't tell her parents as she thought she had imagined the event. The next day the same boy was killed in an accident just at the spot where she had seen the funeral pass. Several days later, my aunt stood respectfully by the side of the road with her parents watching the sad cortège pass for a second time, but this time for real.

Eigg is my personal 'almost disaster' destination. Whilst not on the same scale of severity as my aunt's tale, when I cross to Eigg I find myself in a situation of potential disaster. My first trip there is described briefly in the first chapter about Skye. The second time I crossed was with a fairly large group. We began the trip from the Rhu Arisaig, heading for the south end of Eigg in glorious weather and had an easy crossing. We climbed An Sgurr on Eigg, the shark-fin-shaped blade of rock that gives the island its distinctive profile when viewed from the mainland. Later that afternoon, in fine sunshine, we dropped back down to the ferry tearoom before returning to the mainland. One of our members met an islander whom he knew well who was leaving the island to work in Perthshire. Of course, we stayed for just for 'a quick drink and a hamburger' at her going-away party! About midnight a gaggle of giggling kayakers set off to paddle back in pitch darkness, with only the occasional moonlit break in the thick clouds. We tried to stay fairly tight as a group but in the darkness we began to spread out across the channel. I found myself at the front along with two others. The sea was calm at first but by half way across it was becoming fairly bouncy. One of our threesome was scared as she hadn't been in a sea of this size before. We kept an eye on her as we paddled on. The crossing was particularly slow as we waited for the more hesitant members of the group and by the time we arrived at the cars it was early morning. I was due at work at 9 a.m. but not being fit to drive I slept in the car and made an appearance in the afternoon – knackered. I learned a lesson that night: had any of us capsized in the darkness the consequences would have been very serious.

The third episode relates to a crossing in glorious sunshine, the sea flat calm. After a short break on Eigg we headed due south to Ardnamurchan Point. The passage was easy in the heat of the sun but a long lazy swell came in from the west. I was in a relaxed mode and sat a few hundred metres back from the others in the party. As the boat rose and fell in the swell that was about 5 feet high I began to feel queasy and sea sick. We were about 4 kilometres north of Faskadale and I dropped back a few yards behind the others in the group. I didn't enjoy the passage one bit and was glad finally to set up camp at Sanna Bay that evening.

Here I was again, about to set off to Eigg when within a mile or so the wind picked up from the south making forward progress increasingly difficult. This was followed by the waves picking up to a point where it was becoming uncomfortable. Some of the group were not keen on such a long open crossing in these conditions. We stopped and rafted up to agree a sensible course of action. Mark, Lesley and James opted for the ferry across from Arisaig. Andrea and I decided to continue paddling and to meet the others at the pier on Eigg. This wasn't a good decision. The wind remained fairly steady for the first part of the crossing, the sea a good force 3–4 and bouncy, but it made for excellent paddling. By the half-way point conditions deteriorated; the wind picked up to a force 5–6 and the waves grew from 2-foot chops to 5-foot breakers. The tide was on the ebb and this acted against the wind to make the waves short and steep-faced. Déjà vu, here we go again! The large waves forced us to point our bows almost directly into them to take them head on. This practically stopped our westerly progress towards the island and only on the smaller sets did we manage to make some headway. Although it was hard work, while we had energy we could cope. An hour or so later we realised that not only were we not progressing forward, we were actually travelling backwards. When the big seas had begun we were about level with the village of Kildonan on the southern part of the island; now we were drawing level with the top end of the land and we could see a large part of Rum behind. The southerly waves were pushing us north.

If we continued on this course we would miss Eigg entirely and end up on southern Skye or Soay where we would be unable to contact the others. We closed up to work out what to do and tried to angle our bows more towards Eigg to encourage the sea to make the crossing more like a ferry glide. This didn't work and all we could do was to carry on battling into the sea and managing the odd burst of westwards paddling. My mind firmly fixed on staying upright and in control, the last thing I expected was the appearance of a large grey-black curved dorsal fin that rose out of the water on my right-hand side only a couple of metres away. It appeared for only a few seconds and scared the Hell out of me for a moment. 'Basking shark!' I shouted over to Andrea. We scanned the immediate sea for it and then again it appeared in front of us, surfacing sideways across our bows.

It wasn't a basking shark, however, but a good-sized minke whale, in an investigative mood. For the next ten minutes or more it circled our boats, occasionally running right below us. Even in the rough grey seas we could discern its massive hulk a metre or so under our hulls. I was terrified that it would rise under us and tip us into the rough sea. A rescue would probably not be possible in current conditions and I wished it would move further away. Andrea and I increased our distance from each other in case one was tipped in; we reckoned that the chances of both of us being knocked over were slimmer that way. Our kayaks were over 5 metres long but were dwarfed in size by this amazing creature, which must have been a good 9–10 metres in length. I wanted to take a photo but did not dare to let go of my paddle to dig into my buoyancy aid pocket for my camera. Much to our relief the whale eventually lost interest in us and vanished after one last pass below our boats.

We had now moved a little northwards and were at last gaining some shelter in the lee of the north shore of Eigg. The waves were becoming perceptibly smaller and were losing their ferocity. This, we realised later was because the tide had turned and the forces of wind and water were now synchronised. The downside was that it took an even harder effort to reach the shore on the north-east side. Andrea had run out of energy and to give her a break whilst she ate a snack I put on a tow rope and checked our backwards progress for a while. There was no doubt but that we should have crossed by ferry.

It took another hour or more to cover the last mile to Eigg but eventually we tucked ourselves into a rocky cleft to catch our breath and pluck up the energy and mental resolve to paddle down the coast to the bottom end of the island to meet the others who would be worried about our non-appearance by this time. As we paddled south, conditions improved and by the time we arrived at Galmisdale and the ferry pier, the sun had come out and the wind had almost stopped. The storm which had almost taken us with it had blown itself out. When two shattered paddlers stepped out onto the rocks near to the pier, the lady in the shop was surprised at our arrival; the ferry had been cancelled due to bad weather and she clearly hadn't been expecting any visitors that day. We spoke by mobile to Mark. They would join us the next day, weather and ferry permitting.

More relaxed now, we paddled across the bay to a grassy field and pulled out our large nylon group shelter to warm ourselves – we were too tired to erect the tent – and after food and coffee, slept inside the bright orange shelter for the rest of the afternoon. I was dead to the world. Andrea slept in her spraydeck, cagoule and buoyancy aid – she was too exhausted to remove them. In the early evening we stirred and sorted ourselves out; we changed out of our paddling clothes, set up camp and prepared a good meal of couscous with vegetables and apricots. Shortly afterwards we crawled into our sleeping bags; sleep came quickly.

Much refreshed, the next morning we struck camp, loaded the boats and walked round to the slip to meet the ferry. It was busy with locals and visitors, and lashed to the saloon roof were three kayaks. As it pulled up alongside the slip we stood back against the wall to allow the crew to tie it up. The skipper asked,

'Are you the pair who canoed across yesterday?'

We nodded.

'Well,' he continued, 'I would never have believed that such flimsy craft could make the journey over the channel in the conditions that we had yesterday.'

The weather had taken a turn for the better and once we had unloaded the kayaks from the ferry we retired to the coffee shop to make plans. As this was Mark, Lesley and James' first visit to the island we walked up An Sgurr. The view from the top was staggering. To the north, the jagged outline of the main Cuillin ridge on Skye was pin sharp and beyond we could make out the long punctuated silhouette of the Outer Hebrides. To the east and south the hills of Kintail sparkled with dampness on their rocky flanks and to the west of Ardnamurchan the low shape of Tiree could clearly be discerned. We wondered if we could see a vague edge of the north coast of Ireland, but we weren't sure.

An impressive ring of basaltic column makes An Sgurr appear almost man made. After a while on the summit we dropped down the south side of the escarpment to rejoin the track back to Galmisdale. On the way down we heard a cuckoo call in the distance. Mark imitated it very credibly by putting his joined-hands to his mouth. This then gave way to a staccato avian-human dialogue as the hoodwinked bird became aware of a new intruder (or potential mate) on his territory. Some minutes later two cuckoos appeared above our heads and circled over us while Mark gave it all he could in cuckoo speak. The birds swooped down to investigate, then quickly disappeared. I had never before seen a wild creature responding to an imitation call.

Down on the track we set off to look for Uamh Fhraing, St Francis's

Cave. In the winter of 1577 almost four hundred MacDonalds are said to have hidden in this cave during a feud with their Skye neighbours which began when some McLeods from Skye were sent home castrated as they had been caught raping MacDonald girls on Eigg. The McLeods arrived in force to retaliate. Unfortunately for the MacDonalds, the McLeods noticed footprints in the snow leading to a cave. They tried to smoke out the hiding men by setting up brushwood fires at the mouth of the cave. The tragic consequence was that every single one of the MacDonalds suffocated. To this day, the cave is known as the Massacre Cave. Bones found in it as late as the 19th century were removed for burial. When we found the cave we entered through the narrow opening which widened into a passage that wove a long way into the hill. The memory of its dark history was too much for us. We left silently, lost in our own thoughts.

We cheered ourselves that night by dragging a wooden pallet from the strand and smashing it up with large rocks to fuel a camp fire at the top of the beach near the campsite.

Next day, Becky, a skilful paddler and marine environmental campaigner, joined us and we set off for Rum. We paddled up the east coast of Eigg before crossing the Sound of Rum. Once we cleared the north tip of Eigg we were caught by the fresh south-west wind in the channel. The sea was bouncy and very lively but no more that a force 4 which enhanced the journey across the Sound. We eventually entered Loch Scresort on the east side of Rum. Many years before us, 'The Canoe Boys', Alistair Dunnet and Seamus Adam made this same crossing and faced a grilling by the factor and estate owner for daring to land on Rum. Until Scottish Natural Heritage bought the island in 1957 it was forbidden territory for the uninvited. Visitors are now welcome to the island which is considered one of Scotland's finest nature reserves. We set up camp at the semi-official site near Kinloch.

Rum must be one of the most quirky of the Scottish estates. Following centuries of Norse ownership, the island passed to the Scottish Crown in the 13th century. Centuries later, in 1891, it was sold to the Lancastrian milling millionaire, George Bulloch. Between 1900–1902 he built the massive residence of Kinloch Castle. No expense was spared; the red sandstone was ferried from the Island of Arran and soil was imported from Ayrshire. The workmen were paid extra to wear kilts and given tuppence a day for tobacco to deter midges. The interior furnishings were sumptuous and the splendour extended to heated water tanks full of alligators and turtles. Sadly, this Victorian opulence is slowly rotting away and its present owners cannot afford the cost of fully maintaining the castle. Currently, part of it is used as a hostel and visitors can visit the main rooms. Sandstone buildings, however, if not heated at all times, absorb moisture and eventually dampness pervades.

After setting up camp, I felt tired and slept for a couple of hours while the others wandered around the castle grounds. In the morning we set off to climb the Rum Cuillins, a round of three hills: Askival, Hallival and Trallival, Norse-named summits and ones that we were keen to conquer. As we walked up the first hill we passed through several deer-fenced patches of native tree regeneration. Rum has, for many years, been the location for considerable red deer research. The hills were not high by Scottish norms but were challenging. The last climb up the steep sides to the top of Trallaval was especially difficult. This hill is named after the strange sounds that are emitted from its troglodyte seasonal inhabitants, the marine birds, Manx Shearwaters, which breed in mountain-top burrows. Their ghostly sounds give the hill its Norse name (Troll-i-vall). Dropping down off the hill, the party split into two: Andrea, Mark and Lesley headed back whilst Becky swam in a deep pool in a stream below the hill. James and I wandered until we too were tempted by a dark pool in a stream where we stripped off to bathe our slightly pungent bodies.

Next morning, Becky and James had to return by ferry to the mainland leaving Mark, Lesley, Andrea and myself to carry on up round Rum to head for Canna. The paddle up the north-east side of the island was fine but by the time we came to the north end the wind had picked up from the west and we found it hard going in the rising seas. We struggled with the waves for some time before calling it a day and pulling into the bay at Kilmory for the night. During the evening the wind became stronger and we eventually set up a tarpaulin in the lee of a rocky bluff for shelter to cook our evening meal. As the windy weather was still in play the next morning there was little enthusiasm for carrying on. We made another tentative effort to cross to Canna before turning back and making our way back to Kinloch.

The weather was poor as we sat offshore, rafted together, unwilling to face the long paddle back to Arisaig in such conditions. We paddled across to a large tug which was getting up steam next to the pier and with not a hint of shame we asked if we could scrounge a lift back to the mainland. Although bound for Liverpool the skipper offered to drop us off at Mallaig. Brilliant!

The crew hoisted our kayaks up on to the aft deck and we were off. Mugs of tea and coffee were passed round in the warm galley. In no time at all we tied up to the quay in Mallaig where we were off-loaded. This must rate as one of the best hitch-hiking lifts of all times.

Best meal on trip: stir fry vegetables and noodles

Sesame oil
2 cloves garlic, sliced
2 spring onions, finely sliced
Cube of root ginger, peeled and grated
Medley of vegetables according to taste – mushrooms, carrots, French beans, baby sweetcorn
1 sachet of sweet and sour sauce
1 packet of noodles

Heat the oil until hot. Add all the fresh ingredients. Stir-fry for 5–8 minutes. Add sauce from the sachet, heat through and remove from heat. Cook the noodles according to the packet instructions

The Cuillins of Rum

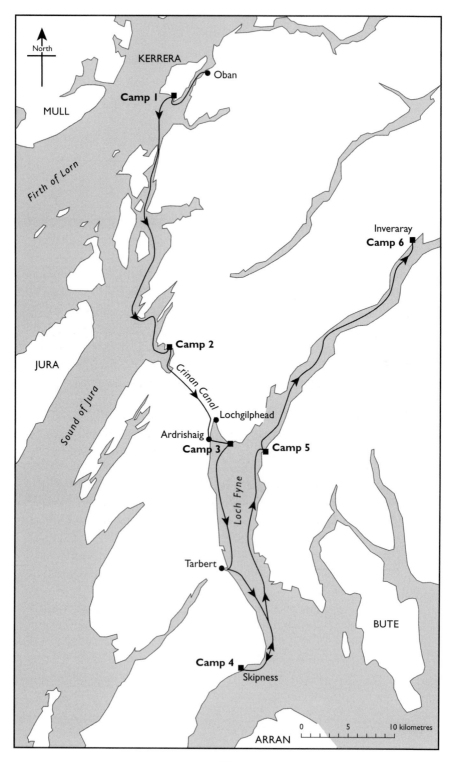

Chapter 7

Oban to Skipness and Inveraray

When we booked our September week's annual leave back in early summer, Mark, Andrea and I had two kayaking routes in mind. The first was to begin at Loch Torridon and paddle north, past Gairloch, little Loch Broom, the Summer Isles, Lochinver, round Cape Wrath and then as far along the north coast as time would allow. This was our good-weather option. The second option, which would apply if the forecast was not too promising, was a bit more vague, but involved heading to Oban and paddling south. With a summer full of work commitments that was as far as the planning went. It wasn't unusual for us to undertake voyages with little or no precise detail worked out in advance. On one occasion the sole planning for a trip from Stavanger to Bergen involved booking the return ferry from Newcastle. Because the weather was favourable, five days after setting off we pulled into Bergen harbour with a day to spare. It almost goes against the 'Zen' of sea paddling to be rigidly timetabled and to be left chasing yourself if wind and sea contrive to spoil things.

The night before leaving, Andrea and I had been at a colleague's wedding. Packing therefore had to wait until morning. Mark, a GP, was in the throes of buying a house and organising a work audit before we met him in Inverness at 2 p.m. on a Saturday in September. We set off, Mark seated in the passenger seat juggling cold pizza, weather printouts and OS maps. Not until we had driven through Inverness did we plump for the Oban option.

We rolled up to Oban's north pier just before 5 p.m. Oban was its usual busy self with visitors wandering to and fro, chips and ice creams in hand. We quickly became the main attraction for an hour or so as we dragged out piles of 'essential' gear and food from the back of the car. Just around the corner of the pier lay the dive charter boat, *MV Kylebhan*, owned and skippered by Jim Kilcullen. During those years when my seafaring was of a different ilk I was a fanatical member of the Perth diving club, and latterly the Inverness Sub Aqua Club. We often went out with Jim to explore the waters around Oban and The Small Isles. The *Kylebhan*'s stopovers in Tobermory were legendary among the diving fraternity. We could never work out why, irrespective of our dive plan or predicted weather, we always ended up in 'Tob' on a Saturday night in the Mishnish Hotel. Usually a noisy, boozy blur led to a sore head the following day, entailing easy diving down the Sound of Mull on the way back to Oban. One year when the stopover happened to fall on Burns' night, we tied up to the ferry pier and even though it was a cold evening, inside the boat's saloon the haggis, neeps and whisky combined to warm our innards. The *craic* was great.

Now, in our smaller craft that were not on the same scale of luxury as *MV Kylebhan* we set to and packed them full of fresh fruit, veg and some excellent wines (not to mention Mark's mead), enough to sustain us in some style for six days. With a disposable barbecue and a bag of courgettes tied to my back deck, we set off, leaving the North Pier and the *Kylebhan* behind. It was just after 7 p.m. and time was short if we were to set up camp below Gylen Castle at the south end of Kerrera before dark. Luckily, the short paddle was easy in the flat sea with little boat traffic.

Gylen Castle, built on a rocky promontory overlooking the Firth of Lorn, has an imposing presence, especially in the poor light of the setting sun over Mull, befitting its chequered and bloody history which includes a massacre of its inhabitants. But for the moment history and foul deeds took second place to our egress from the water in the small inlet below the ruins. First things first: we set up the disposable barbecue to let the charcoal come up to full heat as we erected the tents on the grassy patch just above the high-water mark. Then for some of the joys of sea kayaking: good food, good wine and good company. Tonight on the menu was corn on the cob, red onion, sweet peppers stuffed with soft cream cheese, open cap mushrooms and a whole camembert cheese – all placed over the glowing charcoal embers. Mark brought out a bottle of red wine and we sat in the semi-darkness below the castle looking south to Clachan Sound and beyond, our next day's paddle.

Up and off by 8.30 a.m., we had, as frequently happened over the years, slept through the 5.40 a.m. shipping forecast. Why the forecast cannot be broadcast at a more agreeable time such as 8.00 a.m. is beyond my comprehension. Furthermore, I am still trying to work out why Finisterre has been replaced with Fitsroy in the sea area forecasts. Forecast or not, we were off, and with a north-east wind on our backs we made good time on our short crossing past the mouth of Loch Feochan down to Seil Island, and on past the busy yacht anchorage at

Puilladobhrain. Several yachts pulled out as we approached and one or two even put up their sails. Our short trip 'downriver' through the narrow Clachan Sound was aided by the strong pull of the ebb tide allowing us to drift under the 'Bridge over the Atlantic' before grounding by the famous pub, Tigh na Truish (the house of the trousers). When Highland dress was banned by law after the shambolic Jacobite Rebellion, mainland-bound islanders reputedly halted here to swap their kilts for a pair of trousers.

Seil Island is dominated by the abandoned water-filled quarries, which are a permanent memorial to the many who toiled here over three centuries to produce high quality slate. In November 1881 a ferocious storm breached the main pit, which lay adjacent to the sea, and the water rushed in to fill the 250-foot deep quarry. Fortunately no one was killed but hard times ensued as it stopped the slate business dead in its tracks leaving 240 families without their only means of support. I dived here many a time as the pit was used as a deep diving training site. Several who pushed the boundaries too far tragically died here. The nearby village of Easdale is now dependant upon the tourist pound and is the destination for the many coach loads of human cargo disgorged straight into the art and nick-nack emporium which dominates the otherwise charming village.

Following our brief stop to replenish water supplies, we pushed off again. Andrea made straight for the nearest moored occupied yacht to chat-up the skipper and his two junior crewmembers who were just back from a party in Oban the previous night. Ten minutes later we were armed with the forecast and some good advice on how to negotiate the Dorus Mòr (Big Door), a fierce tide race 20 kilometres to our south and close to the end of our first full day's paddle. In quick succession we pulled past Ardmaddy Castle and Balvicar, across Loch Melfort and on to our lunch stop at Craobh Haven, the rather unattractive purpose-built yacht marina. A check of the tide times told us what we had suspected: our passage through Dorus Mòr was going to fall at the worst time of the tide, mid ebb, but with no other option other than to sit it out, we carried on down the loch, past several large-tonnage fish farms. Like them or loath them, the fish farms have been the salvation of many a small community on the west coast and islands of Scotland.

As we ran out of land to our left on the approach to Craignish Point, rafts of seabirds began to appear, all feasting on the sea life welling up on the now obvious turbulence a short way in front. This brought back memories of a similar experience three months earlier on the trip to the isles at Barra Head. There is always a thin dividing line between really enjoying the exhilaration of a big sea and becoming scared silly. Now here we were again, once more into the breach, lots of birds again meant lots of water movement! A red-throated diver surfaced just off our bows, instantly panicking as we slid past, whilst our minds were now filled with our own silent thoughts. What would appear round the next headland? The Big Door, a very good name for this next piece of sea and according to our tide tables and the advice from the skipper earlier on, it would be firmly closed as we made our approach. The line of turbulence lay in front, running from our left, its source just tantalisingly out of sight, then travelling right across the entire Sound of Jura straight through to the Corryvreckan whirlpool. Suitably respectful, we crept round our first headland to be met with the sight we didn't want to see. From our present position on across the channel from the island of Garbh Reisa almost a kilometre away was a vast volume of water emptying out of Loch Craignish. The water fell by over one metre as it fought its way into the Sound of Jura. The small tree-covered island in the way forced the water into a phenomenal series of whirlpools, overfalls and standing waves.

By now it was getting on in the afternoon and we wanted to make our landfall near to the Crinan Canal before dusk. As there was no place to camp here and we had to get through at some time anyway, the decision was unanimous: push on through. The next small headland was hard work; in a small white water kayak it would have been exciting; in our heavy, less manoeuvrable sea boats there was a high element of risk. One at a time we put on a frantic spurt of speed to gain the slower water on the far side of the rocks. We were now within the door frame of the maelstrom with two headlands to go. The next rocky promontory was more of a problem. Going ashore to view and discuss the passage round we stood right by the water's edge as the full force of the current whipped past the point. It was not possible to paddle against such a force, nor did we want to get dragged offshore into the Dorus where there would be no hope of rescue. We decided to use our towlines to help one paddler at a time to round the point.

Mark volunteered to go first. With me 10 metres upstream pulling on the towline attached to the bow of Mark's boat, Andrea, on the shore, kept pace with Mark, pushing the boat off the rocks as the current forced it sideways with alarming force. Mark paddled and braced like blazes to stop the pull of the towline countering the opposing force of the water which threatened to flip the boat over. After 10 minutes of this and now 100 metres round the point we pulled Mark into slack water and tied the boat up, feeling a mixture of relief and then trepidation for the next person to go through. At this point Mark's awful jokes and patter returned – so at least he wasn't too traumatised by the experience. Me next, with Mark on the towline and Andrea on the rock hopping. From the shore I had been daring, full of confidence and proffered many words of comfort but now in my kayak the prospects seemed significantly different. The rush of water seemed faster, the noise and power of the Dorus took on a more alarming note (as did my heartbeat). I certainly didn't have the easy confidence which Mark exhibited. I felt useless in the boat as Mark pulled; simply trying to keep upright was all I could manage. Paddle flailing on the water and bashing off the rocks did little to aid matters. Mark and Andrea hauled me to safety and I too found my awful jokes and confidence returning in nervous relief. Only Andrea left to go. Her boat was fairly new and we were under strict instruction not to scratch it on the barnacles. The current had abated very slightly and she could assist us by paddling hard. By now we had this towing system cracked and we quickly hauled Andrea round into the bay – gel coat intact. The last small headland to round was not in the same league as the one we had just come through so a hard burst of paddling took us up into Loch Craignish.

Three kilometres to our south-east lay Loch Crinan but before we could finish for the day we had to paddle up Loch Craignish for a couple of kilometres to avoid being dragged back into the turbulence. A quick ferry-type glide across and we landed at a perfect campsite below Ardifuir. A piece of cake! Our first full day of paddling and we now lay just 2 kilometres north of the Crinan Canal and our route through to the Clyde. So far so good.

There were now other important matters to consider: sweet potato, curry, rice and nans, a bottle of Syrah and bizarrely, why you only find left-handed rubber gloves washed ashore on the foreshore. It was time to crash out.

No midges, no rain, no 5.40 a.m. shipping forecast but it didn't matter as the Crinan Canal was not known for its big seas. We were up, breakfasted and packed by 8.00 a.m. Two otters in the bay were also at first feeding. Mark, our resident ornithologist and general avian anorak, spotted a pair of whimbrel on the far side of the bay. For some reason we weren't quite as excited by this as he was. I can, however, now say with some authority that they are similar to curlews but with shorter beaks. They didn't seem to suffer from any diminutive beak inferiority complex and their 'pee-pee-pee' calls shrilled across the bay as we set off to the canal entrance and our passage through to the Firth of Clyde.

Canals are fascinating pieces of living industrial archaeology. The sheer effort of their construction is hard to comprehend; one hundred or so years ago no JCBs or other mechanised help was available to dig and move a vast amount of earth and rock to create them. Shovels and wheelbarrows powered by muscles were the order of the day, as they were to be (less the shovels) for us shortly. Crinan Canal is not very long at 14.5 kilometres. James Watt first surveyed the area in 1771 but it wasn't until thirty years later that it was opened to traffic. It formed part of a vital network of waterways built around the same time. In conjunction with the Forth & Clyde system of canals (the Forth & Clyde, Monkland and Union canals) and also the Caledonian Canal nestling in the floor of the Great Glen, they provided sheltered water communication routes between the east and west coasts at two latitudes in Scotland. The avoidance of the treacherous headlands of the Mull of Kintyre, and to the north, Cape Wrath, allowed cargo vessels to move with ease and safety. At this time there were no railways, and roads were not capable of carrying all of the supplies necessary for the economic growth of the country.

Despite it being a vital gateway to the west coast of Scotland, the Crinan Canal has never become financially self-supporting. Probably by good luck more than anything, the canal is still with us and it now contributes to today's boom in leisure activities and is used extensively by yachts and other small craft. It has had its fair share of calamities over the years. In 1823 when a section of canal bank north of Ardrishaig failed the canal was re-routed to avoid marshy ground. More alarmingly, in 1859, it was necessary to rebuild the summit section of the canal and locks when a reservoir dam burst and discharged a torrent of water, stones and mud débris into the canal. The resultant tidal wave created devastation in its path; locks, paths, roads, and banks were swept away, thankfully without loss of life.

For us, as we made our way to the lock-keeper, the first intriguing event of the day was to see how British Waterways would deal with three kayakers. In true Gillespie last minute 'style' I had meant to phone ahead to check but hadn't. As I had no excuse, the usual 'winging it' rule applied.

Lock keepers appear to be universally unflappable; nothing seems to take them aback or cause them to pause to head-scratch. The keeper at the Crinan office was typical.

'Three sea kayaks? Fine. Pop them in over there and if you sign the insurance waiver then you are free to head through.'

One slight problem was that we could not take them through the locks. Yet, she could not have been more helpful. We were provided with maps and shower keys and lots of advice. And there was no charge. As we waited for the waiver form to be brought from Ardrishaig we had breakfast number two in the coffee shop. Waivers signed, scones consumed and lots of local chitchat, we lowered the boats with towlines into the canal above lock number 14. Only 13 to go! Now, this was something different, inland canal paddling. Earlier in the year we had paddled a few yards along a Viking canal on the Brittle peninsula on Skye. Perhaps we were subconsciously seeking an easier life, avoiding waves and wind.

Our viewing height was rather restricted as we set off along the canal. The canal embankment which we couldn't see over was to our left, and to our right was the rock face where the hill had been cut away. Along both banks were masses of wild flowers and several stops were made to pick ripe brambles along the canal. The journey to Dunardy was very pleasant but locks 13 to 9 were hard work. An empty kayak weighs in at 25 kilograms; our rather full ones must have been in excess of 70 kilograms and not easy to carry very far. Tactic one was to go for a straight portage but even with three to a boat we managed to carry each boat only a few yards at a time before giving up, exhausted. Tactic two involved dragging the boats along the grass by the side of the towpath: again, too hard. This method had previously worked well on North Uist when, to avoid rough seas, we hauled the boats overland from one freshwater loch to the next, the slippery heather enabling one person to pull the boats easily.

On this occasion, however, the grass by the canal was dry and dragging was not possible. Andrea vanished along the towpath to reappear a few minutes later with a black, British Waterways' wheelbarrow, obtained without permission from a lock keeper who had gone for lunch. The contents of his wheelbarrow, paint tins, brushes and signs were now stacked up on the grass at the top of the lock. She left her buoyancy aid and spraydeck as surety for the duration of the operation! What she thought the keeper would do with these is anyone's guess.

Now for portage tactic number three. Which way should we carry the kayaks – across the wheelbarrow or long ways in the same direction as the wheel? Mark was first once more and chose the latter method. Twenty minutes later the deed was done. Andrea and I chose the across-the-barrow-style which was a bit of a hassle in narrow parts of the towpath and also caused great consternation to several passing cyclists. During our comedy portage we were watched with some mirth by picnicking visitors.

When the lock keeper appeared on the towpath after his lunch to find his wheelbarrow missing and then to spot it performing military style manoeuvres with three people and a kayak, we prepared for a good ticking off.

'Are you doing this for charity?' he asked in all sincerity.

A lengthy explanation ensued and we were allowed to finish our portage with the wheelbarrow. Two hours later and four more locks passed, we were off again for the short topmost Letter Daill stretch of the canal before hauling out again for the four downhill locks at Cairnbaan, numbers 8 to 5. Once again a portage was necessary. We had been pulling Andrea's leg about the wheelbarrow 'borrow' and now to her great satisfaction she appeared with yet another (more wobbly) one. The victim this time? The local shopkeeper. By now we were experts at this game and despite wisecracks from passing locals we moved the boats in just one-and-a-half hours.

The launch back into the canal at the bottom of the lock staircase was spectacular. We slid rapidly down the steep grassy bank, then disappeared bow first into peaty water up to the cockpit before the buoyancy of the boats hauled them up again. By now it was 4.30 p.m. and we had been told to make sure that we were out of the canal by the 4 o'clock closing time as it was on the first day of the winter timetable. A fast dash was thus needed along the last few kilometres to get us down to Lochgilphead and the sea. With no more British Waterways' wheelbarrows to liberate we decided not to negotiate the last three locks at Ardrishaig and as the canal at this point runs parallel to the sea we thought that a quick haul over the bank to reach it would be easy.

Andrea climbed out of her kayak and walked along the towpath as we towed her boat until she spotted a suitable break in the canal vegetation near the canal water-level relief mechanism. This is an amazing piece of Victorian ingenuity designed to maintain the canal's water height using a self-regulating system of tanks, balances and plugs. I wondered why a simple spillway at the correct height would not have done the task just as easily. We hauled the boats down the bank and across the busy Lochgilphead to the Tarbert road. Several cars flying round the nearby bend in the road braked hard and swerved to avoid us narrowly.

We clambered down into the sea. The tide was out and the water was very shallow for many hundreds of metres as we made the short paddle across Loch Fyne in the light early evening rain. Steering clear of the local landfill site we pulled up onto a farm track running down to the sea and set up camp. By now the rain was coming down heavily and as Andrea had chilled right down and needed to change Mark and I stayed in our soggy kayaking gear and prepared the *pièce de résistance*: potato and cauliflower curry, dahl, salad and nans, washed down with white wine.

We woke to a foul day: leaden skies, rain and mist. Tents were packed wet before setting off south across the loch. Not quite sure where we were going, we headed in the general direction of Tarbert. Spirits were low; the poor weather seemed to be in for the day (or possibly for the rest of the week). Two hours later we pulled into Tarbert for lunch as a glimmer of blue appeared in the sky. When we paddled past the fishing boats and yachts and up to the slip by the main street we were suddenly the centre of attention. We felt like the 'Canoe Boys' of many decades before whose voyage up the west coast of Scotland drew so much interest. Nowhere before had we arrived to so much attention. Locals and visitors alike were eager to hear of our adventures. The lady from the nearby craft shop took it upon herself to appoint herself chief canoe watcher whilst we dripped our way to the nearest café for food and warmth. Luxurious was the macaroni and cheese with chips followed by apple pie, then a quick strip wash and shave at the loo (whilst jamming the lockless door closed with wellies). Mark popped into the co-op for supplies, as Andrea and I stood respectfully to one side of the road whilst a funeral cortège passed. Remarkably, all but three of the hundred plus mourners on this sombre occasion were men.

Back at the boats, our canoe protector was waiting to assist. She had phoned her husband to instruct him to obtain a weather forecast for us. As he predicted, the sun soon came out and the day was on the up. For the first time on this trip we removed our cagoules and paddled in T-shirts. In the mounting heat we meandered down the coast in no real hurry to reach anywhere in particular. To our right the land rose quickly up a steep slope to about 800 metres above us. The entire length of this escarpment was covered with what must be some of the most pristine natural woodland we had seen. It was sheer pleasure to enjoy some land on which the hand of man had no impact. In the heat of the early afternoon there was little movement or sound. One Peregrine falcon made a brief appearance before vanishing over the heights. Down by the high-water mark a deer grazed, oblivious to our brief intrusion. A string of fish farms lay dotted along the coastal margins which must have been serviced from Tarbert as we could see no shore bases on the nearby coast. To disturb this habitat would be unthinkable.

We were now paddling separately, spaced out by a kilometre or so. The sea was smooth and our only other human contact was a clam diver kitting up to enter the water from the shore at the end of a long land-rover track. On the map, this track began at the tiny village of Skipness, our destination for the day, at the northern side of the Sound of Kilbrannan. The majestic bulk of North Arran lay just 6 kilometres across the other side. It was now late afternoon and the hills and forest had given way to low lying fields and a raised beach as we approached Skipness. Turning into a sandy bay we found a marvellous grassy campsite near to the castle and chapel. On the beach a large piece of driftwood had been converted into a frame for a DIY dream catcher. It was made from lengths of blue and orange twine, shells and bits of plastic gleaned from the beach. As we set up camp our spirits were high and we decided to stay put the next day to take a break from the paddling and to explore the area. Mark's left shoulder was feeling the strain of the paddling and it would do it good to rest up for a while. We settled down contently to our evening fare of couscous (Moroccan style) with apricots, tomatoes and cashew nuts with sweet corn.

A sleep in at last, coffee and bread for breakfast and a chance to do absolutely nothing. In fact the lengthy discussions on what could be done that day far exceeded those for the planning of the paddling trip as a whole. The weather was simply amazing with blue skies and a warm sun and despite the sad memories of the awful events in New York on this date one year earlier (9/11), we were content with life. Gear was dried in the heat, general camp duties performed and a copious amount of good coffee was drunk as we sat on driftwood logs looking across the channel to the jagged ridge of the north Arran hills. We decided not to cross the channel to Arran but to save it for the following year when we could circumnavigate it fully. Mark found an interesting piece of driftwood and proceeded to whittle it into an Easter Island-like monolithic head. We were covered in a breeze-blown stream of wood shavings (which we were still removing from our gear days later) and Andrea was called upon frequently to supply sticking plasters to staunch the blood from Mark's fingers each time his knife slipped.

Later, he popped into the village to post a card and returned with homemade jam-covered cakes bought in the small picturesque post office. If there was ever a requirement for rural subsidies to be targeted it should be for support for these national institutions which are such a vital component of remote community life. Like the 'wheelbarrow' lock keeper of the previous day, the postmaster spoke with a drawl. Trying to stimulate some conversation, Mark inquired if there was much passing trade in the area. 'Only when it is passing, ' was the laconic reply.

Visits to the chapel and castle were next. Both were in a good state of repair. Despite the castle's obvious strategic location at the mouth of

Loch Fyne and close to Arran it had not been the preferred permanent base for many of its owners. Consequently, it would have been attacked less frequently than other castles during power struggles over the centuries. The last call of the day was the plant nursery and the tearoom that specialised in locally caught seafood. This 'exhausting' day was topped with sweet and sour veg, rice and a bottle of red wine.

In spite of a hedgehog disrupting our sleep while invading our food bag in the porch twice during the night we were up early and off by 8 a.m. The weather had deteriorated somewhat as we returned back up the coast for a few kilometres before crossing the mouth of Loch Fyne to Portavadie. Along the rocky foreshore, half a dozen men were bent-double collecting winkles, picking them as fast as possible in the rising tide. As we passed, our greetings were not reciprocated. There was something slightly eerie about the manner in which they turned to watch us pass, pausing momentarily before resuming their picking. The crossing of the loch mouth was made under bleak overcast skies and a mist surrounding us. Despite the brisk force 3–4 wind coming in on our starboard beam from the south-east, the far side was gained without incident.

This, our second last day of paddling, was uneventful. We regrouped just north of the ferry slip. Once again we passed many fish farms looming out of the mist on our way up the loch. By midday we had made good progress and stopped in a sheltered inlet for lunch, after which Mark and I both fell asleep in the now warming day. For some reason we were exhausted. Andrea, very politely, sat around quietly waiting for us to wake up. Later, as the mist burnt off the water, a large grey warship silently slid past and vanished up the loch into the distance. As Mark's arm was still bothering him we called the paddling to a halt at Ballimore just by some holiday cabins. The nearby spit of shingle was covered with many hundreds of oystercatchers noisily squabbling in the afternoon sun. Tonight it was Mark's turn once more to be chief chef and following yet another marvellous meal of risotto and a spice side dish, he set about producing the top dish of the holiday. From the darkest recesses of his boat the bottle of mead reappeared. A bag of pears were peeled and poached in a mix of mead, brown sugar, honey and spices. Topped with Greek yoghurt, this surely was food heaven.

On Friday, and the final day of paddling, the weather changed. A sharp chill replaced the warmth of the previous day. Autumn was in the air as we paddled on up Loch Fyne to Inveraray, our final destination. In the weak sun we were in no rush to finish the holiday and took many opportunities to raft up for snack bars or go ashore for a potter around.

As we approached Inveraray, the warship which had passed the day before was undergoing some spectacular manoeuvres. Between two buoys set 2 to 3 kilometres or so apart, it shot up and down the loch at top speed. Each time it passed, doing 30 knots or more, it sent up a great wash which eventually crossed the loch and rushed up the shore to our left, causing the children playing on the foreshore by the caravan park great merriment as they 'panicked' and ran for the safety of higher ground. When by mid afternoon we arrived at Inveraray we found that there was a dearth of camping places. Not to be defeated, we paddled up the River Aray and set up camp below the castle, tucked behind an area of rhododendron bushes to prevent drawing attention to ourselves. We took a short walk into the village to our last meal of haddock and chips in the George Hotel, washed down with a pint of Guinness. Although good, it did not compare with our own efforts on the Trangia. Still, it was nice not to scrub-out pans in seawater afterwards. A good night's sleep was had by all knowing that there would be no more paddling the following day.

Next morning, in glorious sunshine, we did the grand tour of Inveraray before Andrea caught the bus back to Oban to retrieve the car for the homeward journey and a return to reality.

Kayaking trips can be special for many reasons and this was no exception, but not least for the food, the company and good paddling. That we decided the route as we went along was a bonus. There was never a schedule to follow or a deadline to meet and this, for me at least, was the underlying joy of the holiday. It was wonderful to shake timetabled activities out of our systems, even if it was only for one week.

On our way back up to Inverness we discussed future plans: Arran was a certainty. Islay and Colonsay would also be on the hit list for the following year.

Best meal on trip: pears in mead and honey

4-5 conference pears
1 cupful of mead (brandy or similar if mead is not available)
2 tablespoons of honey

Peel the pears and stand them base down into the pan. Pour the mead and the honey over the pears and cover. Bring the liquid to a gentle simmer for 10 minutes or so until the pears have absorbed the juices and are golden brown. Serve with cream, crème fraîche or yogurt. Wash down with a full-bodied, fruity white wine.

The author and Andrea preparing to enter the Crinan Canal

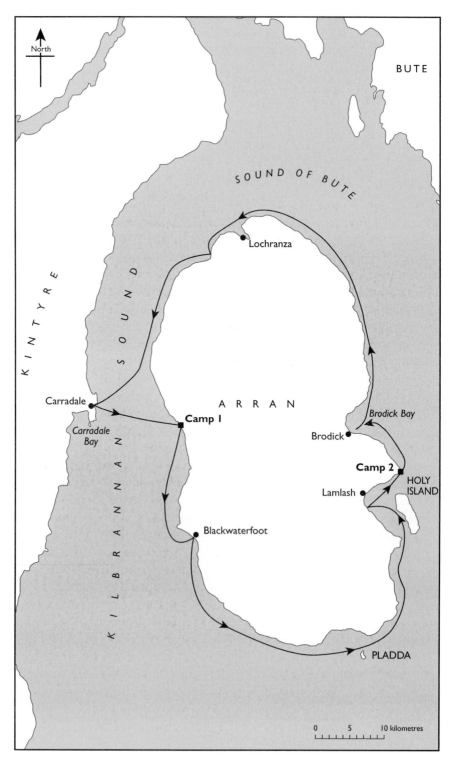

North

BUTE

SOUND OF BUTE

K I N T Y R E

S O U N D

Lochranza

A R R A N

Carradale

Carradale
Bay

Camp I

Brodick Bay

Brodick

Camp 2

HOLY
ISLAND

Lamlash

Blackwaterfoot

K I L B R A N N A N

PLADDA

0   5   10 kilometres

Chapter 8

Mull of Kintyre to Arran

A year on from our Oban to Inveraray expedition Andrea and I made our way down the twisting narrow roads of the Mull of Kintyre to a point a few kilometres south of Skipness from which we could reach Arran from the west. Trying to find a spot to launch along the twisting, tree-lined road from Skipness to Carradale wasn't so easy. One possibility was a fine little hamlet with the odd name of Grogport. We halted for a moment but an old gentleman cutting his grass was less than helpful when we asked about leaving the car. We pushed on to Carradale.

Carradale is an attractive small village whose main road ends at the harbour. This is now a home port to a small number of prawn boats but before the Second World War it was a popular destination for Glasgow steamers. A curious event occurred in this small village on 1 September 1937 which subsequently became known in the press as 'The Carradale Incident'. A local retired ship captain, Angus Brown, set out for a sail in his 15-foot sailing dingy, *The Eagle*, along with his two young children, Jessica and Neil, his brother Robert and a local boy, Donald MacDonald, who helped around the harbour in the summer months. With the aid of a residual swell from a recent storm and a light breeze running from the south the party had made good speed out into Kilbrannan Sound when the main halyard snapped and the sail came down. The two men were annoyed but not too bothered by this hitch, which couldn't be sorted easily at sea, and began to row the boat back the way they had come to the safety of the harbour. Without warning the boat was hit from below and to one side, capsizing it and spilling its occupants into the water. A local boy on the shore recalled seeing a large splash and then the boat being pitched onto its side. In the panic to right the boat and ensure all the children were saved, Angus Brown collapsed and died, probably from a heart attack. His son Neil and his brother Robert drowned in the chaos. Villagers who had seen the event from the shore went to their aid immediately. The local boy, Donald, and Angus's daughter, Jessica, were saved. His brother's body was not recovered for several days. From local accounts it would appear that the tragic event was caused by a basking shark breaching by the side of the small boat, which was not seriously damaged. Had a basking shark deliberately attacked the boat by ramming or landing on top the boat would have been reduced to small pieces. The shark most likely brushed past the boat or its tail flicked it as it rose from the deep to leap out of the water. Breaching sharks had been a common sight in the Clyde in the months prior to the incident and the estuary was said to be 'full' of the creatures. Indeed the fishermen of the area increasingly viewed the basking shark as a serious threat to the viability of their herring fishery and many requests were made to the government to reduce the numbers by any means possible.

A London clerk, Antony Watkins, who was already intrigued by the possibility of starting a commercial shark-oil fishery, read the report of the Carradale Incident in the newspapers with some interest. In the 1930s Britain imported shark oil and Watkins decided that it might be well worth exploiting the large crop of basking sharks for commercial gain. Consequently, in June 1938 he formed the Scottish Shark Fisheries Company, locating its shore base just north of Carradale. Watkins fished during the summer of 1939 and built a factory to process the catch. Following a long interruption due to the war, Watkins resumed shark fishing in 1946, widening his fishing areas and eventually taking in the same waters as the Soay-based shark fishery operated by Gavin Maxwell and his chief harpooner Tex Geddes.

As a boy living on Arran in the late sixties I vividly remember seeing many basking sharks cruising the shallow waters off Brodick and being amazed by their immense size. It seemed to me as though there were two creatures present at every sighting as the dorsal and tail fin were so far apart. My parents once took me and my sisters for a drive along the coast towards the small village of Corrie to see the carcass of a large shark washed up on the foreshore. It did not look like anything I had ever seen before, or since. Its gill covers had rotted leaving the vast head, which was mainly mouth, seemingly separate from the rest of the leviathan-like body of some bizarre sea monster. The awful smell of the corpse could almost be tasted on the tongue it was so pungent. Because the basking shark population declined markedly in the fifties and sixties they are now protected under the Wildlife and Countryside Act.

Whether the actions of Watkins, Maxwell and Norwegian harpoon boats which fished during previous decades caused the decline is not fully known. It is certain that they killed a vast number of the creatures, which were relatively easy to harpoon, as they swam slowly on the surface ingesting plankton, oblivious to the dangers of approaching hunters. Encouragingly, the shark population is recovering and sightings are fairly regular. The Marine Conservation Society website which keeps a database on sightings has provided clear evidence of four 'hotspots' in UK waters, of which the Isle of Arran is one.

With half a mind to keep a lookout for a shark we left the shelter of the small harbour of Carradale just after 6 p.m. and set our course due east aiming to land on Arran at Dougarie before dark. The Kilbrannan Sound from Carradale to Arran is, at this part, only 6 kilometres wide. As we were packing our boats a retired fisherman chatted to us. He was concerned at our plan to cross that evening as the wind was picking up. Having fished these waters all his life he had a great respect for their treacherous nature and said that he would keep a 'weather eye' on our crossing and watch out for our return in a few days' time.

The wind was fairly stiff from the north west but for the first half hour or so the sea was pretty calm. As we left the shelter of the Mull of Kintyre the gusts of wind coming down from the hills made their presence felt. By the time we were half way across the chop was a good size and the boats were surging forward, catching the swell and running down the face of the waves. The only paddle stroke necessary was the occasional dab to keep the kayaks from broaching across the face of the wave as this would slow forward progress. In no time we approached the rocky shoreline of Arran just north of Dougarie Point. Dusk was now upon us and we were not particularly enthused by the prospects of a long paddle in the dark to find the best camping spot: just an easy exit from the sea and a few square metres of grass would do us nicely. We slipped down the coast, staying as close as we dared without getting trashed on the rocks while trying to spot a break in the reefs to land safely.

By the time we were off Dougarie Lodge the terrain appeared flatter and by the boat shed we made a decision to nip up the river mouth of the Iorsa Water, haul out onto the grass above, and set up camp. A family of swans, sheltering from the bumpy seas in the river mouth behind the gravel bar appeared indignant at being displaced from their quiet haven. With much huffing and fluffing of wings the swans swam seaward out to the chop as we slid landward past them. Camp was quickly set up behind a platform of gorse close to the road and an evening meal of pasta and tomato sauce was consumed before retiring to the warmth of sleeping bags and the delights of John Simpson's autobiography on the BBC.

During the last 2 million years, Arran has been repeatedly covered by ice sheets that spread out from the Scottish Highlands. The weight of the ice depressed the land, and Arran was pushed downwards into the earth's crust. Once the ice began to melt, Arran began to rise up again. This uplift, or rebound, has taken place gradually over a period of many thousands of years, and it still continues today. The benefit for the camper is the ubiquitous raised beach which provides excellent camping.

At 5.35 a.m. we were rudely awoken by the mobile phone alarm. The shipping forecast confirmed the reality of the flapping panels of the tent: force 5–6 from the northwest, backing west, then south later. That settled a debate from the previous day: we would circumnavigate the island in an anti-clockwise direction and use the wind to push us south down the west side of the island. Once more we disturbed the swans as we launched in the river mouth. We broke out into two to three-foot-high waves before turning south. The weather was overcast and the occasional shower bounced off our backs as we made excellent progress down towards our first stop to replenish our water bags at the village of Blackwaterfoot. Once again the only part of the foreshore which would afford easy access to the village was at the mouth of the small river. On either side of the entrance, marked by iron rods, were the treacherous reefs. It was crucial not to overshoot these in the surf as we turned in.

Beaching at the side of the small harbour, we dragged our boats out of the water and dug around in the holds for our water bags. It is always entertaining to see the reaction of people when two bedraggled paddlers squelch into a shop or café and ask for water. There's usually a moment of indecision for the owner on whether to accede to the simple request or turn these damp, oddly-dressed persons away. Bags filled, it was back to the boats via the loo and off again onto the sea, which by now was increasing in size and being driven by the wind backing to the west in keeping with the forecast.

We crossed the bay and headed straight for the headland at Rubha Garbhard in order to make some ground before we were driven off the water by the increasing ferocity of the sea. We paddled only a matter of a few metres apart as we alternately rose and dipped either side of the waves which were now running towards us on our right. Close though we were, the noise of the wind and breaking sea made communication almost impossible. We crossed the 2 kilometres of the bay in record time before, a few kilometres further on, swinging south-east and then east to make our way along the south side of the island.

I remembered this part of the island well; as a boy, family outings often took us here for picnics and swims. One such outing ended up with me being taken to the hospital in Lamlash for a tetanus injection as I had a cut foot, the result of an attack by a conger eel, which I swore had lunged at me from its lair under a rock. I was, at the time, convinced of the identity of the perpetrator, but in retrospect I suspect it was a broken bottle and a bit of waving algal frond transformed by the fertile imagination of a twelve-year-old boy.

Numerous volcanic dykes project from the land, the jagged tops of which often lie just below the surface of the water. For some reason the waves were not breaking over them to forewarn us. Even moving further out to sea didn't help and we had a few tense moments as we hurtled down the face of a wave, being driven towards shallow and projecting rocks. Frantically adjusting paddle strokes and swearing, we tensed ourselves for the moment of crunching collision. Thankfully, luck was with us and the thin hulls escaped damage.

By now it was after 12 o'clock and time for food. We tucked into the lee of a particularly large dyke and pulled up for lunch at Torrylinnwater Foot. We found shelter from the wind behind an ageing wood hut filled with rubbish and coated with peeling green gloss paint which flaked off into our tea mugs as we leaned our backs against the wall. Despite the wind whistling around the hut with increasing force we were happy with the progress of the day so far.

'What do you think?' asked Andrea, pointing a finger at the nearby waves with spindrift whisking off the wave crests. It was a question we had asked each other so often: do we go on and battle the elements or give up for the day, set up camp, and relax. We had only covered some 19 kilometres out of the total 100 kilometres for the complete circuit of the island. Although keen as usual to gain mileage I was fully aware of the thin dividing line between an exhilarating paddle and being scared silly and wishing for terra firma and safety. We had got it wrong many times. I knew that Andrea was keen to stop: she knew that I wished to carry on. Even though we did not wish to become stormbound on the southern part of the island we decided to push on for a bit, partly because there were no great campsites obvious in the immediate area of the hut.

Tuna salad rolls finished, it was good to get back into the boats, if only to get warmed up again. To our right in the far distance we could see the rocky outline of Ailsa Craig. Some 8 kilometres away off our starboard bow was Arran's small satellite island of Pladda. We surged forward with the following sea now breaking regularly over the aft deck, running forward, deluging the spray decks and paddler with a noisy swooshing sound. As we approached the Sound of Pladda the waves were concentrated through the narrow channel, becoming shorter and steeper and somewhat more menacing in nature, so much so that we moved northwards from our position in the centre of the channel. There was some psychological comfort in being closer to the Arran shoreline although that had its inherent dangers of jagged dykes to founder on.

We were soon opposite the village of Kildonan and from the vantage point of our bucking craft we watched a bus party potter along the waterfront taking the sea air from the safety of the road, oblivious to our turmoil and constant effort to stop the kayaks broaching in the surfing waves. It was now getting to the point where we were tiring and had had enough. With a measure of relief we shot through the channel and gained some respite in the little bay of Porta Leacach. This heralded the end of the southern part of the island and the beginning of the run north up the east side to our destination for the day at Lamlash. In the space of a few metres we had gone from a stiff sea to a gentle one and by the time we landed briefly at Port na Gallin, it was flat calm.

Our spirits lifted as the sun finally shone and the afternoon temperature rose. We stopped at the small settlement of Largybeg lying tucked snugly below the hills that rose steeply up from the sea. As the houses which lay half hidden beneath the mature deciduous trees dotting the hillside seemed to be unoccupied we nipped ashore for a minute or two. As usual I had my standard soggy beam-end from the poorly fitting spray deck but with the afternoon air now warming in the sun it was time to remove the cags and paddle in light tops.

Paddling on the calm sea was bliss. Conversation soon turned to food and the choice of evening meal. Lamlash, where there was a campsite, was only 10 kilometres to our north. A hot shower was very appealing indeed. Off to our left in the Firth of Clyde we could see the white capped waves still being driven by the stiff breeze. A succession of small yachts fought their way south, heeling over in the wind. An enormous barge that seemed very top heavy with cranes and pipe work was being towed at a painfully slow pace south out of the estuary.

We quickly gained the village of Whiting Bay and followed its long waterfront with what seemed like very slow progress. A youth in a fast inflatable made several passes up and down the bay, each one taking a minute or two to cover the distance from end to end. There are few occasions when I would rather be in a fast powered craft – this was one of them. Tiredness was setting in and with the exception of marvellous views of Holy Island appearing in the distance, this part of the coast was not the most scenic.

Holy Island has had ecclesiastic connections since the 6th century when it was home to one of Columba's disciples, St Molias. The hermit lived on the island, reputedly to a ripe old age of 120, in a cave which still exists. In more recent times the island has been bought by the Samyé Ling Tibetan Buddhists whose twenty-year plan for the island includes the construction of cells to provide retreats for a 200-strong community. The monks have worked hard to turn the island into a place of worship, peace and meditation and have embarked on a programme of reforestation. Parts of the island are set aside for animal and bird life and despite the terrain looking rather barren, a herd of wild goats and soay sheep roam freely on the hillsides and the lower slopes offer enough pasture for highland cattle, ponies and of course rabbits. The island to the south rises in sharp profile to a height of 314 metres providing valuable protection to mariners seeking safety in Lamlash Bay.

Kingscross Point was our next headland. From here it was a sharp turn to the west, the entrance to Lamlash Bay and the end of the first day's paddle. Andrea was flagging a bit (as I was too) as we slogged against the afternoon breeze to cover the last few kilometres. I was happy to be in front as that would afford me time to locate the campsite. The tide was falling as the foreshore at Cordon, to the south side of Lamlash, approached. Unfortunately, the nearest I could get to the part marked on the map as the campsite was a couple of hundred metres. I beached the boat and trotted up the foreshore to seek out the site but to no avail. After much struggling amongst the brambles and scrub along the top of the beach it quickly became obvious that the campsite was neither accessible from the sea nor could even be seen behind foliage and a row of houses. By the time I had walked back to my kayak the tide had dropped further and it took quite an effort to drag it back to the water's edge as Andrea arrived.

'It's not possible is it?' came the dejected rhetorical question. There was no option but to set off again round the bay to find a spot clear of the village. Passing by my old secondary school brought back many memories. I remembered that we had one slightly 'alternative' art mistress who drove a tatty old open-topped ex-US army jeep with great aplomb. We would often gather by the spot near the school wall where she always parked, pocket money ready to make bets as to how close she would park to the wall as she braked the vehicle to a screeching halt. Normally she would gauge it to perfection, leaving a space of only an inch or so but on odd occasions it would go wrong and the wall would be rammed with a mighty thump. No matter, she would hop out and swoosh off to the staffroom without a glance back at the crowd of spotty kids arguing over who had actually won that day's bet.

Bizarrely, one day as this ritual took place and she had just walked away from the jeep we heard a high-pitched whiz over our heads followed straight away by something impacting into the school wall and then falling to the playground. We picked up a rifle bullet with flattened nose! We looked around to see where it had been fired from but there was no sign of the offender. One of my classmates put it in his pocket as the bell sounded and we didn't think much more of it. It now strikes me as odd that we didn't report it; had the shot been a couple of feet lower one of us could easily have been killed. The school's rector was a fairly stern man and I can only suppose that no one had the courage to approach him – even when shot at! Interestingly, I have no memory whatsoever of a classmate who would become a Scottish First Minister. I don't suppose Jack McConnell has any memory of me either!

The inshore part of the bay north of the school was festooned with boats at anchor and quite a few members of the local yacht club were out in their dinghies for some early evening practice as we threaded our way with some caution. The Holy Island ferry emerged from the pier and lost no time at all in getting 'on the plane' and surged past bearing two orange-robed monks across the bay to the religious centre. Normally we would have lingered to enjoy the atmosphere of a busy anchorage but by now our sole aim was to set up camp, eat and rest. It was not until we had left the village behind us that we managed to finish the day's paddle at a small bay called Kerr's Port, just short of Clauchland's Point, beyond which the coast turned westwards into Brodick. From there we would commence the northern half of our journey the following day.

We busied ourselves hauling out the kayaks and searching for a decent bit of field, not too pock-marked with hoof depressions and cow pats, to set up tent. The journey around Lamlash Bay had taken the best part of two hours which was slow by anyone's standards but we were pleased with the overall progress of the day. Having circled half the island we could now relax and consume our meal of quorn sausages, beans and reconstituted potatoes. Perhaps not much had changed from my school canteen days here some thirty years previously. Certainly, to us that evening it was a veritable feast and I amused myself wondering what my former classmate, Jack McConnell, was eating that night. To cap it all we decided to wander down to the village for a pint of beer in the nearest pub. There are times when simple pleasures are all that are required after a long day in a soggy kayak.

We woke early again, firstly to the sound of the alarm and shortly afterwards to the whooping and calling of a girl herding the cows in for milking from the next-door field. From then on until we left at around 8 a.m. a steady stream of dog walkers traipsed past the tent along the path to the headland. Most were friendly enough, as were a pair of hyperactive spaniels snuffling about in our piles of wet gear. One odd character passed by with barely a nod. He was carrying a knapsack over his shoulder from which emerged a cable to join up to an 'H' shaped antennae-like device in his hand, presumably some sort of tracking device. We kept an eye out for him as we rounded the point but he was soon lost in the undergrowth somewhere.

The morning air had a damp chill about it although the forecast was fairly good, with light winds and some hope of sunny intervals. Once launched, we quickly rounded the point and the broad expanse of Brodick Bay immediately opened up in front. Across the bay the red sandstone of the Brodick Castle caught the first of the sunlight and heralded the promise of a good day's paddling. A short distance beyond the point we came across a cormorant with one wing caught on a fishing hook on a line which was attached to a small plastic buoy that was part of submerged fishing gear. As we approached, it tried to dive but the float forced it up again. After a bit of a chase we managed to free it from the line and float but the hook was too firmly embedded in the wing to release. The sea bird was strong and difficult to hold still, especially as it was making a concerted stabbing attack on our bare hands with its sharp beak. We had to let it go. It flapped off a short distance before diving below the surface; whether it would survive or not we didn't know. The line of floats marking the fixed lure lines continued on for the next few kilometres. The glinting lures a few metres or so below the surface of the sea were highly visible in the clear shallow water. We wondered how many seabirds were lost as a by-catch to this fishery.

By the time we neared Brodick the weather had sorted itself out and the day turned into a stunner, with blue skies, bright sunshine and flat calm seas. I had been back to Brodick only twice since I left in 1972 and on both occasions I was surprised at how little it had changed. One thing we did notice, however, was the wind-blown mess of a landfill site near the pier. Plastic débris was strewn all along the foreshore and crowds of gulls wheeled raucously above. Surely in this day and age we should not be depositing our domestic waste in landfill sites; this one did not even seem to have a liner to help to contain the waste liquor.

We drew past the ferry pier which was exactly as I remembered it all those years ago when many an evening was spent dangling a Woolies-bought fishing line in the sea, hauling out mackerel by the score. Once when an eider duck went for my lure it proved to be my biggest ever 'catch'. A crewman from the ferry helped to land it and release the lure from its beak. My other memory of the pier was of watching an episode of Para Handy being filmed. This was the original TV adaptation of Neil Munro's novel, *The Tales of Para Handy*, with John Grieve as Dan McPhail, Walter Carr as Dougie, Alex McAvoy as Sunny Jim and Roddy McMillan as Para Handy himself, captain of the fine vessel, *The Vital Spark*. The climax to the story was Sunny Jim perched on a luggage trolley thundering down the hill from the cottage hospital, along the pier, through a pile of fish boxes and then over the edge into the sea.

With 'more steam McPhail' for us we powered the last few metres to the shore and then squelched off for coffee and a cheese scone at the nearest café. The slog of the previous day was now firmly behind us and after the break the paddle out from Brodick straight across the bay was amazing. The sea was as flat as the proverbial mill-pond, apart from the wash of the Ardrossan to Brodick ferry arriving with the usual CalMac flat-out speed which was held until the very last moment. The ship then swung round to a shuddering stop at the pier, inch-perfect as always. Perhaps it was being piloted by my old art teacher who had moved on from her jeep days?

Merkland Point drew past and marked the start of the run due north to the top of the island. Just to our left ran the road round the island, following the raised beach but hidden from us by the thick alder woodland. The next 6 kilometres to Sannox were stunning. The sea was so smooth and clear that every sea creature and frond of kelp could be seen easily below the boats. We dawdled along in the afternoon sun, startling surfacing seabirds as we slipped along with little reason to make us hurry. We passed the houses at Corrie before coming upon a small sandy beach just past Sannox Bay which was perfect for our lunchtime haul out. An added bonus at this point was a Forestry Commission car park and toilet block just metres away over a small river. It was a perfect place to lunch and have a quick wash, both body and smelly clothes.

As we sat on the picnic benches a French youth was trying hard to launch himself into the air with a parafoil wing. Several times he gathered himself and gear, ran down the short length of grass towards the sea to stimulate some airflow to loft his wing and himself upwards. His rather bored girlfriend watched with an air of resignation, like us, knowing that it was a bit futile in this still late-morning air. We wondered what he would do even if a breeze did catch and allow him to take-off; the only places to land, other than the patch of picnic-area grass were the forestry plantation behind or the sea. We left him to his antics, packed our stuff away and paddled on, with the occasional backward glance just in case a sea rescue was required.

The coast road left us at Sannox and took a short cut over the hill to Lochranza at the north of the island. From here up to the Cock of Arran only a footpath picked its way along the coast below the impressive escarpment above. This was obviously a very popular walk and we watched people making their way along the path. We deliberated over a proposal, published in the local press, to develop a set of fish farms along this part of the coast and decided that it would be a severe intrusion on this marvellous remote, very tranquil part of Arran. Whilst I am a fervent supporter of the aquaculture industry and all the benefits it brings to the economy of Scotland, there must be areas which are off-limits and which can be retained as havens for people, visitors and locals alike. Perhaps there should be Special Areas of Conservation, not just for the protection of rare birds, dolphin or obscure marine invertebrate, but also for another stressed species – mankind.

It was around 2 o'clock in the afternoon when we rounded the northern part of the island at the Cock of Arran; the weather was holding and we were good for many more kilometres yet. One plan discussed earlier in the day was to pull in at Lochranza and camp by the castle. If we carried on down the west side of the island, judging by the map, suitable camping areas would be limited. Just off Newton Point we were still tempted to finish the day's paddle, laze in the afternoon sun and potter round the village. I also had half a thought to try to find the oddly-named rock formation near to Lochranza known as 'Hutton's Unconformity'. James Hutton, a Scottish geologist, noticed in 1787 that rock strata at Lochranza which inclined nearly vertically was overlaid by another almost horizontal rock strata. He had previously discovered similar formations at Siccar Point on the Berwickshire coast and eventually concluded that the layers of the lower strata of schist had been tilted and eroded over a long period of time before the upper strata of sandstone had been deposited on top of it. From his observations Hutton formulated the Uniformitarian theory of geology, and proposed that the earth was much older than hitherto considered.

We decided that geology could wait until our next visit as with only 16 kilometres to go, the lure of completing the circumnavigation of Arran that day was becoming too great to ignore. Conditions were perfect and we were enjoying paddling along the beautiful coastline. Andrea's only proviso was that we stop for food. A hotel was marked on the maps just past the village of Catacol. A short paddle later we beached the boats below the hotel on some kelp-covered rocks and trekked up the grass to order a plate of chips and two glasses of orange juice. We joined several groups of late summer holidaymakers on the wooden benches on the hotel lawn to enjoy the sun and keep an eye on the boats below.

Replenished and back on the water, we paddled on, now running down the west side of the island past Pirnmill and on to the part of the island furthest west at Imacher Point, a couple of kilometres from our point of arrival a day or so previously.

With a right turn, we began the crossing of the Kilbrannan Sound back to Carradale. The paddling was easy going in the flat sea and as we approached the harbour, a fishing boat gained on us and slotted itself in between the handful of other boats already moored, the crews sorting out their catches. From the boats came a call and the fisherman we had spoken to at the beginning of the trip was surprised to see us so soon.

'How far round did you paddle?' he asked and was intrigued to hear that such small craft could circumnavigate the entire island in such a short time.

Now that we had 'checked in' with our fisherman friend we packed our gear into the car and set off to the nearest campsite for a welcome shower and bar meal in the local hotel.

Best meal on trip: basic vegetable curry (best with two stoves)

Root vegetables: e.g. potatoes, carrots, turnips, sweet potatoes.
Cooking oil
1 onion chopped
1 garlic clove, crushed
1 teaspoon ground cumin
1 teaspoon ground coriander
1 teaspoon turmeric
1 teaspoon chilli powder (optional depending on taste)
1 tin chopped tomato
1 cupful of basmati rice

Peel and chop the vegetables into small cubes. Place in pan with water and bring to a rolling simmer to soften. When still slightly undercooked take the pan off the heat, cover and place to one side. Bring rice to a gentle simmer for 5–10 minutes. Remove from heat and place to one side to finish cooking. Fry the crushed garlic and the chopped onions in oil until soft. Add the spices. Fry for a further 30 seconds or so. Add the drained cooked vegetables and the tin of tomatoes and bring to a simmer for 5 minutes. Remove from stove and reheat the rice.

Lamlash Bay and Holy Island

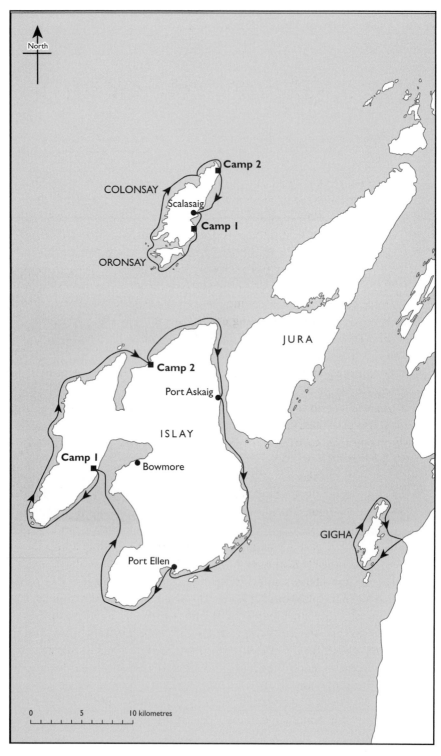

Chapter 9

Islay, Gigha and Colonsay

The forecast was good for a week's kayaking round Islay, the southermost island of the Inner Hebrides. Although the island lacks the stunning mountain scenery of Skye and Mull, its history, as well as whisky and birdwatching, endows it with considerable importance. From the 14th to the 16th centuries much of the west coast of Scotland was governed from Islay by the Lordship of the Isles. The origins of the Lordship date back to the defeat of the Danes off the coast of Islay in 1156 by Somerled, the then military and political leader of the Scottish Isles who was known as the King of the Hebrides. By the 14th century the Lordship of the Isles, Clan Donald, had become so powerful that it conducted its own affairs and made treaties with England, France and Ireland independently of the rest of Scotland. The clan's seat of government was in the north of the island at Loch Finlaggan. Amazingly, this important historic site was virtually forgotten about and was only extensively excavated for the first time in 1989. Now, however, there is a charitable trust to promote the island's antiquities and to provide a learning centre for visitors.

Our ferry to Islay arrived mid-morning at the small town of Port Ellen. We carried the boats off the car deck and launched at the nearby slip into the harbour. The skies were overcast in battleship grey and the wind was force 2–3 from the south west. We slipped quickly out of the shelter of the bay past the long line of skerries before crossing to join the south coast of the Oa peninsula by the lighthouse at Carraig Fhada.

We had had a busy summer kayaking and Andrea and I felt fit as we paddled down the pleasant, but not spectacular, coast. An hour or so later we approached the small headland at Rubha nan Leacan where the sea had flattened and the sun was making its first appearance of the day. I stopped paddling for a moment or two about 100 metres from the shore for a drink and a quick snack. Andrea was about 50 metres further out. As I looked round towards the shore, I seemed to be moving past it at a rapid rate of knots that was most unusual. Just at that moment, Andrea shouted a warning and looking forward again I could see the outline of a row of standing waves a couple of hundred yards in front. Horror! These were pretty big and we couldn't see what was beyond around the corner. By the time we decided to turn back and go ashore for a recce we were almost upon the tidal rip. I had initially tried to back-paddle as I reckoned that by the time I made my long turn in the heavily laden boat, I'd be upon the rip and travelling sideways to boot. Even while paddling hard backwards with a ferry glide towards the shore, I was still bearing down hard upon the turbulence. Andrea had peeled off seawards and was slowly struggling her way round to escape the worst of the tide and to retrace her trail back to safety.

In panic, I made a frantic dash for the cliff just before the little headland and the tidal rip converged. Using the speed of the current to help me get towards shore I reached the rocks just in time and with the bow about to hit the cliff, I made a pretty desperate high brace, leaning the boat hard to make the stern catch the current to assist it in the turn. I clattered against the rocks, but at least I was facing back the way we had just come.

The paddle back to re-join Andrea was more sheltered and I could fairly readily overcome the near-shore current. We paddled apart for 300 metres back up to Carraig Bun Aibhne and met at the point where Andrea found a cleft in the cliff that she had noticed earlier in passing. It was just wide enough for our boats and we gratefully bumped up the gravel shore to catch our breaths. We walked along the cliff top down to where we had turned back to see what conditions looked like from above. I was immediately struck by its similarity to the Point of Neist on Skye. There was a wide, fast-flowing river of sea water heading west with a series of standing waves on top caused by the westerly winds – not a good place to paddle into.

I nipped back to the boats for food and a folder of information for tidal calculations. Everything I needed was there in the hold. For Shetland! I had packed the wrong books.

Despite Andrea's obvious disgust at my inability to get this simplest of tasks right, she ate lunch and snoozed while I checked the speed of the rip at regular intervals until it looked viable. When we eventually re-launched we bumped over the waves without too much difficulty. Ironically, this wasn't the scary current mentioned in the books – the books lying at home in the cupboard!

Once clear of the current our paddling settled to a nice easy pace again but we were still in a state of heightened awareness as we made our way along to the Mull of Oa. The rocky cliffs were high and indented with clefts forming an impressive frontage for the island which faces defiantly into the might of the Atlantic's winter storms. Many sea vessels have foundered on the south and west coasts of Islay when caught in terrible weather conditions or trapped by the ferocious tides that sweep past the Rhinns and the Mull of Oa. We had heard stories of treacherous conditions at this headland. With nowhere to land, it was all or nothing. As we paddled close to each other we looked up to the cliff top far above us where we could just see the monument erected to commemorate the loss of the *Tuscania* in February 1918 and HMS *Otranto* the following October.

The *Tuscania* had crossed the Altantic with a complement of nearly 2,500 US crew and troops bound for the trenches of France. As they approached the waters of the North Channel they were being followed by the German submarine UB77 commanded by Captain Wilhelm Meyer. When he attacked the ship, two of his torpedoes raced harmlessly past but the third made a direct hit. Despite assistance from three escort destroyers, the *Tuscania* slowly sank beneath the icy winter waters with the loss of 230 men.

HMS *Otranto* collided with HMS *Kashmir* on 16 October 1918 in poor visibility and rough seas. She was holed on the port side forward and, in the heavy swell, began to list. The stricken ship then hit rocks and became grounded. With the heavy seas pounding her continually against the rocks the ship eventually broke up and sank with the loss of 431 lives. The destroyer HMS *Mounsey* came to the rescue but as the waves were so big it was extremely risky for the smaller ship to come alongside the liner to take off troops. The ships came together four times and each time hundreds of troops jumped across the heaving gap. Many were crushed between the hulls or drowned.

As we arrived at the Mull of Oa the seas were kind to us and we rounded the headland without incident. We could now relax and enjoy the afternoon paddle up into Laggan Bay which stretched out for eight kilometres before funnelling us into Loch Indaal to the north. Islay is virtually split in two by this shallow loch with attractive sandy beaches along its shores.

It was late afternoon by the time we approached Laggan Point and the narrows of the loch. We had planned to finish for the day at Port Charlotte on the other side of the narrows, only a few kilometres away. There was only one slight problem: the weather had changed and a thick sea mist descended reducing visibility to less than 50 metres. Here came my second disaster of the holiday: I had forgotten the hand-held compass! We decided to paddle up the east side of the narrows to minimise the crossing distance and also any chance of colliding with other vessels. When we calculated that we were directly opposite the far shore we turned 90° to the land and set off into the mist. I am well aware that what we were doing goes entirely against all established navigation and risk assessment protocols. We knew the risks we were taking but nevertheless reckoned we would be fine.

We paddled in heavy silence, partly because I was in the dog house for the second time that day, but mainly because we were intent on listening for approaching vessels and for cars or people on the other side to guide us to the shore. It is a strange sensation paddling in heavy mist and we hoped no-one else would be stupid enough to be out on the water that afternoon! Within 40 minutes or so we made it to the other side and emerged out of the mist only a few hundred metres south of the village of Port Charlotte and the youth hostel where we planned to stay over for the night. Day one: a piece of cake!

The warden lived up to his reputation of being friendly and helpful. He allowed us to set up tent in the grounds and to use the hostel facilities. We presented him with a photograph some friends had taken of him a few weeks before. Once showered and changed we enjoyed the evening in the warmth of the commonroom, reading the hostel's supply of local guide books and old *Cosmopolitan* magazines. It rained through the night and as the sun hadn't risen above the hill by the time we set off to dry the tent, we packed it wet.

The paddle down the low coast toward the Rhinns was straightforward. The weather was bright and the sun shone strongly between the broken clouds. The warden at Port Charlotte, who had encyclopaedic knowledge of recent disasters and people lost at sea while travelling round the point at Rhinns, had offered helpful suggestions. Having been caught out the previous day we tried to get the timing for going round the point correct, and for once we managed. As we turned right round the headland the island of Orsay came into view a short distance away. The sea was bouncy and confused, even during a period of slack. The paddling was great fun in this lively, but gentle sea and we were soon in between the Rhinns and Orsay. Pleased with ourselves, we stopped for a break at the pier below the village of Portnahaven. Here we experienced a strange feeling, almost as malevolent as that at Rodel on Harris. It was as if the village was waiting for something to happen to make it come alive.

Our journey up the southern half of the west coast of Islay was uneventful. At one point we passed a concrete structure with a big dark slot built into the rocks; I assumed that it was a wave generator but didn't venture too close to check. So relaxed were we that our thoughts turned to future trips. The coast at this point reminded us very much of the outer islands of the western fjords of Norway which we experienced the previous year while paddling from Stavanger to Bergen. We had enjoyed this immensely and were keen to explore the coast north of Bergen.

We stopped at Machir Bay for a snack and a stretch. Here on a beautiful surf beach we were alone – not a living soul in sight. Such a real sense of remoteness pervades the western coast of this small island on the south-western extremes of Scotland and no great distance from Ireland that it is hard to believe that the island's population is around 3,000.

The coast changed subtly as we re-launched and rounded Coul Point. There were now endless sea stacks and underwater reefs which we had to watch out for when the swell dipped to expose kelp-covered rocks. Our sense of wellbeing over the previous few hours was suddenly shattered. Andrea was paddling just a metre of so in front of me off my right-hand side. From out of nowhere a massive wave grew rapidly to our immediate seaward side, developing right under us. I was thrust up its face, bracing wildly. I pushed my paddle blade deep into it to keep my balance. A second later it picked Andrea up too, leaving me a good metre or more higher than she was on this freak wave. At its peak we could see below and slightly in front of us a big black rock as it was uncovered by the water being drawn up into the wave. By now the wave was a good 4 metres high and about to break over the rock. Frantically, we both made one-sided stabbing paddle strokes forward along the face of the wave to clear it before it exploded down on to the rock in an almighty crash. The outwash picked up the sterns of our kayaks, thrusting them forward. We surfed and braced hard for many metres in the froth. It was all over in seven or eight seconds.

Looking back at where we had just come from, apart from a dying ripple on the surface, we could see not a trace of this wave from nowhere, nor any sign of another. It had happened so fast that we burst out laughing with relief and surprise. We looked back several times over the next half an hour until we turned the next corner but saw no sign of a breaker like this one. Were the gods trying to tell us something or simply reminding us who was in charge here?

By lunchtime we were off the north coast between Nave Island and Ardnave Point and it was here that we came ashore for a long lazy lunch stop above the beach. We had now come away from the exposed west coast and were running along the top end of the island with the sea behind us. Happy with our progress, we aimed to set up camp early, allowing our wet tent from the previous night to dry quickly in the afternoon sun. As we set off again, the vast sandy expanse of the entrance to Loch Gruinart at low water lay off to our right, pock-marked with seals enjoying the warm afternoon sun. We were in no hurry to reach the opposite shore in those magical moments of sunshine on clear blue water showing off the changing sea floor beneath our boats.

Coming towards land again past Gortantaoid Point we spent some time choosing the best place to go ashore. The rocks here formed a seaward curtain of clefts and arches, behind which was a series of small sandy beaches with grassy hillocks above. We found a cleft through which we could slip over a rocky lip to pull up by the beach. Twenty minutes later the tide dropped below the lip, cutting the inlet off and leaving an ideal large natural swimming pool for washing away the grime of the day's paddling. The tent draped over the rocks was soon dry. We sat in the warm sunshine working out tides and timings for the next day when we would be turning south into the Sound of Islay between Islay and Jura. This sound runs at a fair old speed at mid ebb on a spring tide. When I last sailed down it by kayak, one of the members of the group with a GPS unit recorded 11 knots as we sat rafted together in the tidal race – and that was without paddling!

That evening, after our meal, we wandered back along the coast to the big beach at Tràigh Baile Aonghais where we sat watching the sun go down, turning deep blood-red as it slipped into the water on the horizon. This had been a good day of paddling, not least because of the excitement of the freak wave on the west side.

The good weather continued the next day and we were off once the rising tide flowed into our sea pool. We had 10 kilometres to run before joining the Sound of Islay. Off to our left we could clearly see the island of Colonsay only a short distance away. We were tempted to turn north to it but if the weather changed we would have difficulty getting the ferry back to Oban and catching a bus to Kennacraig to retrieve our car. It would be best to bide our time and try for it later.

According to our calculation the tide was at its highest as we entered the Sound of Islay which would allow us to ride the ebb south once the tide had turned. In the event, we were half way down the sound before the ebb picked up to give us an advantage. Consequently, we stopped at Port Askaig to let the tide gather some strength. We pottered around for an hour or so, buying postcards, replenishing our water sacks and watching the Islay to Jura ferry slide sideways back and forth between the two islands. Once we could see it sag into a loop as it crossed the sound we knew that the tide was running hard. We set off again and made easy progress down the bottom of the channel before pulling into the remarkable bothy at An Cladach.

The bothy sits by the sea and although it takes a good walk by hill track to reach it over land, by sea it was a dawdle. The building was last lived in by 'Baldy Cladach', an illegal whisky distiller who was removed to the Americas in 1850. The ruin of his house was renovated by the Mountain Bothy Association in 1999, the visitors' book testifying to its comfort and popularity. From it the views south across to the Mull of Kintyre were wonderful and we could just make out the hills of North Arran on the far side.

Now that we had lost the assistance of the ebb flow the next 12 kilometres were tough going. By the time we had arrived at the bottom end of the east side of the island we were tired and looked for camping sites with little success. When we reached the bottom right hand corner of Islay I realised that it was only another 12 kilometres back to our starting point at Port Ellen, and if we carried on at our present pace, we could catch the afternoon ferry back to the mainland. By so doing new possibilities for the remainder of the week would open up. I didn't voice these thoughts as I knew Andrea was tired, as was I, and continued looking for a good spot to stop for the day. I should have known better. Andrea knew exactly what I was thinking and had already resigned herself to the last dash for the ferry.

The passage along the south coast back to Port Ellen was very satisfying and the best part of our coastal vogage. There were many small islands and channels to head through, albeit with the occasional blind alley to catch us out. At one point we squeezed through the shallow channel by Eilean Mhic Mhadomhòire where we came across a large fish basking in the warm shallows. It took fright at our approach and we followed the wake of its dorsal fin for many metres as it frantically tried to find deeper water to escape. The water was just deep enough at the shallowest part of the sound to pass over in our kayaks. On the southern end of the island five deer were grazing which, at our approach took fright, and swam across the channel in front of us at quite a surprising speed.

In no time we were abreast of the offshore island of Texa and making a final run into the ferry terminal at Port Ellen. We had a pleasant tour round the town which seemed a little down at heel as though its glory days had been and gone some decades before. We bought a few supplies and wandered back to meet the ferry coming in. We strolled over to a bunch of paddlers who had come off the boat but as they didn't really engage with us, intent on getting under way, we left them to their preparations. Had I been in their situation I would have been keen to pick the brains of those who had just completed the circuit for good places to camp and things to watch out for.

We boarded the ferry and headed back to Kennacraig. True to form, CalMac provided the best possible plate of macaroni cheese and chips. It was good to get a carbohydrate overload.

That evening we camped at Rhunahaorine, right by the sea and across the short channel from our tent was the island of Gigha. This was too tempting and as we had a day in hand, the next day's destination was quickly determined. We were both tired but content that evening, having paddled for three days, 55 kilometres that day alone.

There was no great need to be up and off early to catch a tide or ferry. The sun was strong in the clear blue sky and it was a pleasure to sit around the tent for a while enjoying the warmth on our backs. The sea was glassy calm and we watched the small ferry running to and from Gigha. It was a perfect day for a day paddle with near-empty boats. Gigha was only a few kilometres away across the shallow sound and we headed off at a diagonal route to run straight to the southern end of the island, cutting behind the ferry as it passed over to Gigha.

We tucked in between the southern tip of Gigha and its southern outlier, Cara Island. The west coast of Gigha was rocky and enjoyable. Two thirds of the way up the west side we came to the shallow indentation in the coast of Port Bàn. In 1991 the Russian fish factory ship, the *Kartli*, was making her way south homeward bound for Bulgaria with 51 crew on board. Off the west coast of Islay she was caught in a violent storm and a freak wave hit the vessel amidships smashing into the bridge and flooding the engine room. Three of the crew in the bridge were killed instantly as the structure collapsed on top of them and a fourth person died later in hospital. After the remaining crew were rescued the abandoned vessel drifted in the storm and eventually went aground at Port Bàn. The ship was subject to a spate of looting, particularly of the electrical goods that the crew had bought to take home. It lay where it sank for two years but the hull eventually broke up in the continually pounding seas and now all that we could see were a few bits of rusting steel lying jammed in some rock crevices.

The sun was blazing down on us when we pulled into Bàgh na Doirlinne where we lingered for a long time, savouring the beauty and tranquillity of the island. From here is was only a few minutes paddle up to the north end of the island followed by a leisurely potter down the east coast before heading back over to the campsite on the mainland. The whole circumnavigation had taken just 5 hours. It had been a perfect day trip indeed with good weather throughout.

On this, our second night at the campsite, we lit a disposable barbecue on the sand dunes in front of the tent. We sat long into the evening cooking bits and bobs gleaned from our depleted stores, sipping wine and watching the rich red sun slip silently down behind the crest of Gigha. It had been a day to savour for a long time to come.

Next morning we packed and set off to Oban to replenish our food and drink supplies before catching the ferry to Colonsay, the next island on our itinerary. We popped into Nancy Black's, the chandlery in Oban, to check out the coastal pilot notes for Islay. We were quite taken aback at the advice for Mull of Oa to Rhinn's Point. 'Keep at least five miles to seaward unless in a big boat, especially in a flood tide.' It had been a flood tide we had encountered at Rubha nan Leacan! Suitably shocked, we went for coffee before preparing the kayaks once again for the ferry, which arrived 40 minutes late, having gone to the assistance of a stricken yacht.

The ferry threaded through the marvellous islets of the Garvellachs. The sea was flat calm as we joined other passengers on the outside deck to take pictures and enjoy the passing scenery. Andrea then bumped into a minister from her old church in Macclesfield. He and his wife were doing 'locum' for the Colonsay minister whilst he was off on his own holidays. Although the size of the ministerial flock was small, Colonsay and its small neighbour Oronsay which are joined by a tidal causeway, are steeped in religious significance. On Oronsay there is a ruin of an Augustinian Priory dating from 1380 which is second in importance to Iona. The tidal causeway between the two islands, known as The Strand, has a cross half way across it. Legend has it that any Colonsay fugitive who reached this cross was immune from punishment provided he stayed on Oronsay for a year and a day. In the extreme north of Colonsay, set in a low valley, lie the remains of Catherine's Chapel, which may have been built on the site of a 13th century convent.

When the ferry pulled into the pier at Scalasaig at 7.30 in the evening we wanted to find somewhere to set up camp fairly soon. Not knowing how welcome casual campers were we were a little wary of onlookers as we carried the kayaks down to the water's edge. A local fisherman encouraged us to camp wherever we wished. In the end we camped in the next bay south of the ferry pier at Loch Staosnaig, which was at least out of view of houses and enquiring eyes. It was only a short walk back over the low hill for a quick pint that evening and to check out the weather for the next few days.

The hotel was quiet but we got in tow with a retired fisherman who was 75 years old but looked not a day more that 50. He was from Lybster on the north-east coast of Scotland and when we mentioned that we had once canoed into the harbour there he recounted many amazing tales of storms, big herring catches and wild nights in the fishing bothies. Like many fishermen, he was sad that the days of a vibrant fishing industry were over as the fish stocks had collapsed all round the coast. The fishing station in Lybster was now a café and heritage centre. As we walked back to the tent we could see the blink of the Islay lighthouse at Rhuvaal which marked the entrance to the Sound of Islay where we had paddled only a few days previously.

We were up and off by 8.00 next morning. There was a stiff north westerly wind blowing over the island, but we were relatively sheltered on our paddle down the east side. We quickly covered the distance to the bottom end of Colonsay, passed the causeway and stopped for our first break on Oronsay. We pulled out below an interesting stone cottage, named Seal Cottage on our map. It was a holiday cottage and peering through the window we could see that it contained some amazing home-made furnishings. Seats and tables were made of driftwood and there were glass fishing buoys strung up on the ceiling like giant Christmas decorations. In front of the cottage lay a large tubular buoy that was clearly a scientific sonde which had been washed up or caught in a fishing trawl. I wondered who owned it and I was sure that whoever did would be very glad to get it back again.

Back on the water again we soon reached the south end of Oronsay. It was quite difficult to negotiate the tip as it was scattered with shallow reefs. We grounded again on the beach next to Dubh Eilean to visit the remains of the priory, crossing grassy fields to the buildings ahead of us on the highest point of this low-lying island. A farmhouse built with stones removed from the priory lies immediately adjacent to the priory remains. However, there was still a lot of the original series of chapels and associated buildings remaining. There was also a 3.7-metre high Celtic cross on a low mound standing next to the old cloisters. At the time of our visit The National Trust for Scotland was conducting renovation work and much of the area was covered with a lattice of steel scaffolds wrapped with tarpaulins flapping in the wind.

As we paddled north up the west coast from Oronsay we were exposed to force 4 winds. The sea rolling in from the north west made for hard work and slowed down our progress considerably. When we were about half way up the coast we pulled into the bay of Port Mòr, just south of An Rubha. We were both tiring and needed a rest from the incessant oncoming waves. We rafted up and ate some food behind a large rocky promontory. A creel boat pulled in behind us, drew level and then hove too. It was the fisherman whom we had met the previous evening at the ferry pier. He had given up fishing for the day as the sea was becoming too rough to work his pots safely. He wished us well and motored over to his mooring further into the bay. From our map we could see that it was another 6 kilometres to Kiloran Bay where there was a good campsite. By now the wind had dropped but the sea was still running head on to us. It took over two hours to paddle to Kiloran where we surfed ashore for lunch, huddled behind a large rock inside our nylon group shelter in an attempt to warm up. We were in no hurry to move on in the lumpy sea caused by the tide working against the prevailing winds. Having snoozed for an hour or so in the shelter we went to check the sea. What a difference! The sea was now half the size it had been earlier. Encouraged, we pushed on to round the north tip of the island in the hope that we would find shelter on the east side.

As we approached the northern tip the sea became very rough between the north headland and the little off-lying islet of Eilean Dubh. We pushed through a series of large steeply-faced waves that rebounded off both sides of the narrow channel before reaching calm seas on the east side. Rafted up again for a quick snack we were surprised by the frantic flapping of a juvenile gull's abortive attempt to land on our heads.

Gull-less, tired, and late in the afternoon it was time to stop for the day. We were exhausted by our efforts on the west side, but happy with our overall progress that day. We had paddled almost the entire circuit of the two islands. We eventually found a wonderful sandy beach 1 kilometre south of the northerly tip, the only place to camp before the ferry pier and our starting place. Backing the beach was a long row of large sand dunes. We dragged our boats up the beach and set up the tent in a grassy depression in the dunes.

Refreshed from our meal we wandered up the hill to see the remains of Catherine's Chapel. Searching in the bracken, we came across the low stone rectangle of the chapel. At one end we found a large squared-off stone with a small smooth font carved out of it. A few metres away there was a short three-quarter-metre-high Celtic cross, sitting a little off the vertical, smooth and polished from endless generations of animals rubbing themselves against it. It was difficult to comprehend why these important ecclesiastic artefacts have been left unprotected and lying around to act as sheep back-scratching devices. We sat for a while on the little hill above the chapel absorbing the serenity of our surroundings and watching the last of the sun sinking behind the distant clouds.

The paddle down the east coast back to the ferry pier the following morning was more than pleasant with the sun warming our backs as we went. An hour later we drew up to the slip and dragged our boats to the small coffee shop at the top of the harbour.

As we had a few hours to spare before the ferry would leave we walked to the gardens at Colonsay House, now occupied by the son of the 4th Lord Strathcona and his family. Mostly planted in the 1930s, the garden has some of the finest rhododendrons in Scotland, azaleas, magnolia and some exotic species from the southern hemisphere. We spent a marvellous hour or two alone in the gardens meandering along the paths and by the ornamental ponds. It was hard to believe that we were on a remote Scottish isle and not in a warmer climate such as the Scilly Isles. I remembered once hearing that many of the tree ferns first introduced to this country were transported from New Zealand with their root balls wrapped in Hessian and frequently dampened with water on board the ships. Contained within these root balls were a species of terrestrial amphipod (a sand-hopper-like creature). My search around the roots of some ferns in search of these alien creatures was sadly disappointing.

As we arrived back in Oban late that night at pub closing time the chaotic and violent scenes along the main street as drunks dodged boy-racers in their souped-up cars, or argued over nothing, was a rude shock to our systems and a far cry from the peace of Islay, Gigha and Colonsay.

Best meal on trip: cauliflower curry

1 medium cauliflower, cut into small florets.
Cooking oil
1 onion, finely chopped
2 cloves of garlic, crushed
2 teaspoons ground cumin
½ teaspoon chilli powder
1 tin chopped tomatoes
1 cupful basmati rice

Fry the cauliflower florets in the oil until brown and then put aside. Fry the onion and garlic until softened and turning brown. Add the cumin and fry for a further minute. Add the chilli and fry for a another minute. Add the tin of chopped tomatoes and the cauliflower. Mix gently. Cover and simmer for 10 minutes, stirring regularly. Place the rice in a pan and cook. Reheat the curry if necessary. Serve with yoghurt, mini nan breads and red wine.